Edw[...]
Lake Placid, NY
Summer, 2008

# TRUE SPIRIT, TRUE SELF

## EDWARD O. WELLES

Vital Mind Press

*To Eddy and Hugh*

---

Copyright © 2005 by Edward O. Welles

Cover photo by the author
Cover design and layout by
In the Woods Design Studio, Lake Placid, NY

All rights reserved. No part of this book may be reproduced in any form whatsoever without permission from the Publisher, except in the case of brief quotations used in critical articles or reviews. For information address:

Vital Mind Press
P.O. Box 483
Lake Placid, NY 12946.

To purchase additional copies or for bulk sales contact
Vital Mind Press at www.vital-mind.com

ISBN 0-9765734-0-7

First Edition

10 9 8 7 6 5 4 3 2 1

# CONTENTS

| | |
|---|---|
| Preface | vii |
| Introduction | ix |
| Chapter 1. The Ground of Personal Mastery | 15 |
| Chapter 2. The Nature of Belief | 33 |
| Chapter 3. The Self in Action | 49 |
| Chapter 4. Relationships | 79 |
| Chapter 5. Making a Living | 101 |
| Chapter 6. Crafting a Life | 117 |
| Afterword | 137 |
| Suggested Reading | 139 |

*Nothing so much diminishes not only happiness but efficiency as a personality divided against itself. The time spent in producing harmony between the different parts of one's personality is time usefully employed.*

— Bertrand Russell
*The Conquest of Happiness*

# PREFACE

This book first took shape as a letter addressed to my older son on the occasion of his 21st birthday. I considered it a father's prerogative – and privilege – to pass along a few ideas that might serve his son as he came of age.

As that letter evolved into this book, I realized that I might be writing something for a wider audience. I hope this book will resonate with readers at various stages of life, whether they are embarking on a career, contemplating new directions in midlife, or deciding how to best apportion their energies in the later years.

This book is intended as a guide of sorts; call it an "owner's manual" for the 21st century citizen. We live in interesting, albeit complex times. We should do our best to both enjoy and survive them. One idea that may come through to readers in these pages is that we humans, for all our intelligence, can often be contradictory creatures. We say one thing and do something else, often to our eventual regret. Accordingly, one aim here, conceptually at least, is to forge a unity between thought and action in the service of the happy life.

This book follows a simple format. It is meant to flow from the inside out, beginning with the conscious self. It leads from there to the realm of ideas and belief, before breaking through to the outer world of daily life where we put our values into practice, relate to others, and ultimately make our way by the work we do and how we do it.

This book is intended to be accessible in the best and fullest sense of that word. It is written to be read in a single sitting, or, conversely, considered a page or two at a time. I hope this book might become a good companion, to be readily consulted by the reader for counsel he will find as sound as it is surprising.

E.O.W.
Lake Placid, N.Y.
May, 2005

# INTRODUCTION

There is an essential duality that underlies and defines every aspect of life. Good opposes evil, night becomes day, and the masculine sensibility complements its feminine counterpart. In a similar vein, people can be divided – broadly speaking – into two different groups.

The first tends to seek comfort, fear failure, and resist change. Its members may crave power for its own sake, grasp for undue advantage, or engage in other obsessive behaviors, both large and small. In sum, their lives are out of balance. Life, when all is said and done, happens to them.

The second group, a relative minority, displays a more organic, intuitive feel for life. Its members see life as a *process*, requiring initiative and effort. They understand that risk, struggle, and failure, even, are woven into the rhythm of existence. Looking forward, not back, these people act with a confidence grounded in trust. Generally asking less of life, they stand to receive more.

It is our collective fate to be born into the first group. We begin as creatures of sense and appetite, but one reason why we are here is to transcend our basic wants and move to a higher plane. We are here to evolve, and in so doing cross the divide between the netherworld where instinct rules to a loftier realm where awareness informs action. How we make this transition is the subject of this book.

Moving from a life that is reactive, fearful, and uncertain to one that is intentional, positive, and fearless is no mean feat. Where, in fact, would a person even know where to begin?

One response to that question – as rational and western as it is spiritual and eastern – is that we begin where we are. We live in a society that celebrates status, wealth, and fame. The broad cultural messages we beam – emphatically – at one another typically imply that leisure is a worthy end and that success is most genuinely defined in material terms.

If we find such messages to be misleading or inauthentic then the appropriate corrective is to embrace their antidote. Court some discomfort, eschew luxury, measure achievement by the quality of your effort, not the size of the reward. Craft a well-considered philosophy of life, and don't let the values of the herd sway your thoughts or dictate your actions.

We can only grow when we accept – and even welcome – a certain measure of discomfort. That does not mean we should intentionally court undue pain or privation, as that, in fact, is the surest path to misery. What I suggest, rather, is that we begin to live sound, full lives when we venture forth, moving away from what we find too easy, safe, and familiar, and take on endeavors that test and stretch us. Only then do we rouse the potential within. Only then do we waken the spirit and stir the soul.

# INTRODUCTION

After graduating from college, I, like many others at that juncture in life, was uncertain about what I wanted to do. A succession of short-term jobs leading more or less nowhere ensued. But in time, something inside me of was beginning to point toward true north. I wanted to become a writer.

But the only way I could make that happen was by, in fact, becoming a writer, not just posing as one. What mattered was taking action; following through, no matter the attendant uncertainties. That required that I save some money, quit another job, buy a secondhand car, and take off. I traveled alone for four months and 8,000 miles around the country, with the express purpose of writing a book on the America I observed in my journey.

In retrospect, outsiders probably concluded that I was heading off on a quixotic journey. (The notion certainly occurred to me.) Yet, I knew that the path to my becoming a full-time writer could only lead through the *completion* of the journey. That consideration trumped all doubts. It meant that when my car broke down for good in Utah I wouldn't just fly home or hop a bus. I sold it to a pawnbroker for $125 and then used the proceeds to buy a backpack, sleeping bag, and pocketknife. I was thus ready to hitchhike home the remaining 2,500 miles.

The slog back east provided its share of discomfort, as I found myself sleeping in dark fields, marooned on lonely stretches of highway, and catching rides with my share of desperate, if not scary, strangers. Still, that trek proved to be the easy part. Once I got home that fall and drew a breath, I moved to a small town in New England, where I forced myself each day to sit down at my typewriter and complete the journal I had set out to write.

## TRUE SPIRIT, TRUE SELF

Closing the deal and finishing the job, no matter how discomfiting to spirit, ego, or flesh, created fresh openings in my life. It led the following spring to my first paid work as a magazine writer, which led from there to a 25-year career as a magazine journalist, the last dozen of those as a senior writer with a national magazine.

In truth, the discomfort has never really gone away, and that may not be all bad. Practically everything I have written for publication over the years has brought on gnawing feelings of doubt as I churned my way through the reporting and writing. But on the other side of each published story I have also felt a calming sense of proficiency that has emboldened me to take on and finish the next assignment.

I recently dislodged myself from my comfort zone, leaving magazine journalism for personal coaching. The latter is probably as ill-defined and uncertain as my original road trip, three decades ago now. But I felt that it was time to move on to new work that would challenge me as journalism once had. I also realized that, having seen another 30 years of life in the interim, perhaps I had developed some insights that could help others.

In the process of making this change, I also moved from a somewhat predictable life in a big-city suburb to living at the edge of a mountain wilderness within the six-million-acre Adirondack Park in northern New York. With only 150,000 full-time residents in this vast space and few meaningful jobs to be had, it's a situation that encourages, if not demands, that a person create his own line of work.

As inconvenient and unsettling as these changes might be,

## INTRODUCTION

they have forced me to reconnect with my essential self – doubts, fears, and all. That is hard but healthy work because it is through awareness of our true natures that we express our fully authentic selves to the world. It is only then that we begin the noble work of crafting lives that are mindful, optimistic, and fully intentional.

People who live these traits are generally happier, healthier, and *freer* than their counterparts. They understand that it is only through conscious, spirited effort that we take our lives to life and in the process open the door to fresh, great, and sustaining possibilities – awareness, happiness, wisdom, love, and joy. They show others a way through, inviting them to venture forth and revel in the bounty that beckons.

CHAPTER ONE

# THE GROUND OF PERSONAL MASTERY

**Find the Flow of Life**

Evolution, as articulated by Charles Darwin, is one of the big ideas of modern times. All things shift. All things change.

But in thinking of evolution, many of us mentally separate ourselves from the idea in order to distance ourselves from death. In fearing our future demise we'd rather not acknowledge our present frailty. Instead, we tend to think of "nature" as the realm of plants and animals. We do not perceive ourselves as the human animal, and we see evolution as a theory, and not a dynamic physical process to which we so integrally belong.

And so we often resist change, to our passing confusion and ultimate chagrin.

A happy life owes to its willingness to accept change. We are here to find life's flow and work with it to get to where we want to go. We are here to push ourselves forward and advance our lives. We are here to evolve, and if we don't muster the courage to create that positive energy, then life, in all its weighty certainty, falls back on us.

## TRUE SPIRIT, TRUE SELF

We evolve – and lighten the load – by turning our energies to fruitful, creative ends. This idea struck me recently while reading a newspaper article about postwar Afghanistan. A semblance of civic life had quickly returned to the streets of Kabul after the Taliban's fall. Museums, shops, restaurants, and hotels had reopened. Commerce and culture were beginning to stir.

This was the scene after the Taliban's rigid rule had effectively consigned the country to a stone-age existence for a generation. In their deep, regressive resistance to any outside belief, the country's theocratic rulers had bequeathed the country an unhappy legacy in the form of the severe oppression of women and an abidingly cruel intolerance. The physical manifestation of this was nothingness, rubble; a beautiful country and culture turned into a soulless void.

The message here is a forceful one. When we live as evolved, unfearing human beings we welcome and work with the constant of change. We harness its energy and turn it in our favor. We transcend conflict, whether that's between or within us. The harmony that naturally results fosters a creativity that sustains and nourishes us. We forge a virtuous cycle that is as pleasurable as it is productive.

### Quiet the Mind to Open the Senses

Living a life that is open to change enacts a life that is open to possibility. We create fresh perspectives we could not otherwise imagine. Ideals such as wisdom and truth come within reach and into focus. We turn them into practical ways of living.

Wisdom is about consciously getting in touch with the quality of experience. It is not about the obsessive gathering of knowledge. It is about gaining awareness; quieting the mind in order to open the senses. Wisdom occurs when we take authentic (truthful) actions. It is as much bound up in how I peel an orange as how I consider my existence. Wisdom is not a prize to be gained at the end of a contest but a process that gets you into a boundless game. It's a way to live your life. And we gain wisdom by readily opening ourselves to the flux and flow of life.

### Truth is Focus

All we really have is our lives, but we often don't treat them as the precious, unique things they are. Life gets away from many of us as we surrender our best days to lesser pursuits. We turn worrying about the wrong things into a comfortable habit.

This is the central conundrum of being human. We are here, ostensibly, to live, but we settle for survival. Our lives begin to hollow out. They feel inauthentic.

Pursuing truth offers a way back. Truth is not just a concept; it's a force. It is any thought or act that cultivates awareness. The more aware we become the more readily we can focus on those things that matter, and relinquish those that don't. As we sharpen and strengthen that focus, our goals begin to come within reach.

Focusing on worthy goals helps a person set a course in life. It reinforces considered thought and direct action. Assuming more ownership for, and authorship of, our thoughts makes us more responsible in our actions. As we assume more responsibility for who we are and what we do we deepen awareness, the fertile ground of truth.

## Build From Your Inner Blueprint

For life to play out the way we fully intend we should think of it as having a coherent plan. Each of us carries an "inner blueprint" which imparts a sense of order, progression, and continuity to our lives. Through conscious thought we uncover that plan and allow it to inform the course we follow.

We might think of life as comprised of stages, or chapters. Each unfolds naturally into its successor and builds on what has come before. Typically, a well-lived life might break down into four stages. These phases of life comprise a coherent progression that provides order and meaning. They are:

1. Education: Becoming enlightened.
2. Apprenticeship: Valuing work.
3. Craftsmanship: Finding true success.
4. Mastery: Gaining wisdom.

Some observations on the above would include:

*Education is a lifelong process because we are always at risk of descending into darkness.* Many people live their lives in retreat or without a plan because they fail to see the value of education, and thus the organizing power of the mind. Their lives often lack form, energy, and direction. When we are willing to open ourselves to learning, we open ourselves to the daily truths of what surrounds us. We instill in ourselves a bias to openness and lightness. Our prevailing direction in life becomes "up" and "out." We push, like plants, toward the light.

## THE GROUND OF PERSONAL MASTERY

*Value apprenticeship.* Apprenticeship, in its most sincere form, honors what we do. It is humility in the service of craft. In our society, too many of us violate the spirit of apprenticeship. We are in a hurry to make money and seize the low-hanging fruit of status in lieu of the enduring rewards that proficiency confers. Many people become nominally educated, earn a degree, and gain a credential, yet they still lack a true mission in life. Many "well-educated" people in our society – so-called professionals, even – can be out of balance due to an exaggerated sense of self-importance and a consequent grasping after status or riches that throws them off kilter. Their ability to "command" respect diminishes their prospects of earning it. But when you value apprenticeship you push a spirit of learning and inquiry into all corners of your life. Wonder, which always renews itself, becomes your guide and reward.

*See craftsmanship as true success.* Success, as we know it, is generally about making a certain amount of money and achieving a certain social rank. It is something that provides status. It is a measure of attainment and says little about how we arrive. When honestly pursued, craftsmanship signals that we have taken our apprenticeship seriously and value our work for its own sake. We simply commit to doing a good job. There is no division between ego and labor; we fully invest in what we do. Craftsmanship has little to do with success in the conventional sense. It is really about being responsible to, and for, our work. The sense of proficiency we gain in the process makes us responsible to others and to the world at large.

*Mastery is happiness in action.* Committing to lifelong learning and practicing humility and commitment in the service of craft prepares us to receive wisdom. There are no shortcuts. In completing our work, we complete ourselves. We live whole and happy lives, which speak for themselves. They never require explanation to others, nor to ourselves.

### 'Assert Consciousness'

Any important undertaking flows from the core of one's being; the sensibility a person brings to the task. The right sensibility is rooted in the urge toward self-knowledge, or in what psychologist Nathaniel Branden calls "the will to understand," which he sees as vital to high self-esteem. In *Honoring the Self: The Psychology of Confidence and Respect,* Branden writes: "The beginning of self-assertion is the assertion of consciousness itself, the act of seeing and seeking to grasp that which we hear – of responding to life actively, not passively. This is the foundation of honoring the self."

The early Roman philosopher, Seneca, put it another way in *Letters from a Stoic.* "Carry out a searching analysis and close scrutiny of yourself in all sorts of different lights." Knowing oneself is not egoism, nor narcissism. It's a selfless undertaking that will set you apart from the crowd and set you on a higher course in life.

As Branden suggests, self-awareness forms the ground of a purposeful, energized life. Consider the example of Michel de Montaigne, the 16th century French thinker and writer. After a life in the public eye, Montaigne deliberately withdrew during his final 30 years. In relative solitude, he chose to write about what he knew best – his own thoughts, habits, and opinions. "My trade and art is to live my life," he wrote. "The man who forbids me to speak of my experience, feelings, and practice of it might as well forbid an architect to speak of building."

Montaigne's keen regard of self served as a well-polished prism through which he viewed life. Common sense, a self-deprecating humor, and a sharp eye for human virtue and foible alike were his trademarks. He favored the sensible and unadorned over the contrived and pretentious. As Montaigne's life, which combined simple pleasures with mental rigor, showed, we become comfortable with life as we grow content in our own company.

The man who shuns his own companionship is ultimately a lonely man because he risks estrangement from himself. Even worse, he is often inclined to export his inner tensions and conflicts to the lives of others. Conversely, the man who keeps mindful company with himself dwells in a resonant solitude. A yearning to be with the crowd often bespeaks a fear or dislike of one's self. But when we readily seek our own companionship, we do so with the assuring knowledge that we will never be alone.

### Practice Forges Identity

"Self acquaintance is a rare condition," writes the noted art teacher, Robert Henri, in his classic, *The Art Spirit*. What makes it so?

Adequate self-knowledge requires both honesty and sustained effort. There is always more to know about oneself, and we can't stop in that quest. It's easier to delude ourselves about who we really are and seek shortcuts. The problem with that strategy is that shortcuts often turn into dead-ends.

## TRUE SPIRIT, TRUE SELF

The best way to avoid that pitfall and embark on the vital work of self-discovery is to turn life into a series of "practices." Take on every task with a certain degree of devotion. Whether you're reading a book, playing a sport, doing your job, or just doing the dishes, flex your consciousness so that you fully inhabit and explore the moment and space you inhabit. The more your mind comes in active contact with the realm it happens to be operating in, the more opportunity there is for identity to form.

Thirty years ago, when I set out to become a magazine writer I started reading the masters of the craft. One of my earlier influences was *The New Yorker* writer, John McPhee. I admired the care McPhee took in putting his stories together, his fluid prose, and seamless craftsmanship. I read interviews with the author describing his interviewing technique and his habit of covering a bulletin board with carefully arranged three-by-five-inch notecards bearing salient ideas from his reporting before he even began the writing process.

McPhee's first contribution to *The New Yorker* was a 1965 profile of Bill Bradley, the former U.S. senator, who at the time was an All-American basketball player at Princeton. The title of that piece was "A Sense of Where You Are," and it emerged from McPhee observing Bradley's ability to shoot certain shots without facing the basket. As he told McPhee, "When you have played basketball for a while, you don't need to look at the basket when you are close in like this. You develop a sense of where you are." In one scene in the book, Bradley, after missing a few shots in practice in an unfamiliar gym, told McPhee that the basket was "about an inch and a half low." McPhee later went back with a step lad-

## THE GROUND OF PERSONAL MASTERY

der and tape measure. He found the basket to be an inch and an eighth below regulation height.

Bradley's discipline in practice resulted in his being a scoring machine in games, when it was routine for him to pour in 40, or even 50, points a night. (The same can be said of McPhee, whose legacy of care for his craft 40 years later is a body of highly-regarded non fiction.) We might say that such productivity was founded on Bradley's sheer faith in touch and eye, and a keen sense of his position on the court.

Through his awareness of where he stands, the confident man's surroundings reflect back truthfully to him. He internalizes a realistic – not a warped nor delusional – sense of his environment. Bradley, self-conscious in the best sense of that term, subsequently went on to a life of accomplishment in other arenas. After his All-American career at Princeton, he was, successively, a Rhodes Scholar, a professional basketball player, a U.S. Senator, and a candidate for the presidency.

Aware people tend to be accomplished people, and vice versa, because they strive to see themselves as truthfully as they see the world around them. Armed, like Bradley, with this reliable sense of both self and place, they develop a quiet self-confidence. You cannot gain the latter without the former. To know where you want to go you must know where you stand.

Like Bradley on the court, we are more likely to succeed when we recognize the signposts, touchstones, and borders that demarcate the arenas we play in. And then, reliably orienting by them, we forge identity through sincere and steady practice. As we build self-knowledge at the core and a reliable universe at the perimeter, distractions fall away. We frame our lives, clearly and cleanly, by understanding what matters and what does not.

### Pay Attention

A sure identity allows a person to move out from a well-developed core and come to know the world. Self-awareness, a source of abiding inner strength, comes at no price. It is free in objective, monetary terms, a deep reserve available to us at any time. The cost is simply a commitment to the idea that any undertaking, no matter how seemingly mundane, has the potential to teach us something about ourselves, provided we accord it sufficient respect.

Self-knowledge springs from paying attention; consciously looking in order to see. It's engaged openness.

As a professional journalist, I have had the good fortune to be paid to listen to others and be curious about their stories. I have entered private worlds and asked questions of otherwise perfect strangers. Along the way I have met Nobel laureates, common criminals, billionaires, and ballplayers.

In the process, I discovered that most every person I met had something to teach me. Listening to others for a living taught me a respect not just for the ability to listen, or the need to listen, but the *pleasure* of listening. Listening clears a space for silence, which is the ground of empathy, another core attribute of the evolved person. Once you have that habit in place then curiosity will flow. And the more curious you are the more receptive and teachable you become.

The self-aware person has quieted his ego and transformed

it into a consciously observant state. He makes no special claims or boasts because he is mindful that knowledge, like the energy of the universe, is eternal and shared. The wise man avails himself of knowledge, as though he were drinking from a mountain stream, and not feverishly digging his own well that may some day go dry. He does not lay special claim to knowledge because he understands that the more open, selfless, and ungrasping he is in receiving it the wiser he becomes.

### Happiness is Depth

The ability to quietly observe and carefully note is tied to our capacity for happiness. Happiness is the quiet joy that comes when we are able to see clearly into life. It transports us past the surface of things to those places where life unfolds and yields its secrets. Happiness pierces the veil of ignorance. It takes us beyond pretense, posture, and fear, delivering us into the depths of wonder.

We begin life as superficial beings. We live on the surface and relate to the world one dimensionally. Superficial living may be "easy" as it requires our fleeting attention, and, therefore, little effort. But its net effect is to deflect and dull us. It diverts us from seeking the deeper meaning of life, and if we cannot penetrate the ground of experience then we struggle to root our thoughts and feelings. "The mind that skitters only on the surface is easily distracted, for it doesn't see enough detail or subtlety to hold its attention," writes Tim Gallwey in *Inner Tennis: Playing the Game*. "Unable to remain focused on a single object or activity for long, it is unable to sustain interest in learning because it cannot penetrate the nature of things, where the real interest lies."

When we are ungrounded we often feel unsteady and unsure of ourselves. In the face of such uncertainty we often simply yield and live lives concerned mainly with appearances. But when we do that we risk paying a future price in the form of pain we struggle to absorb. Conversely, the more we cultivate the ground of self, the more we prepare ourselves to sustain and fathom whatever shocks life sends our way.

### To Live Living is to Live Right

It is this quality of depth and cultivation that distinguishes the evolved, authentic person. What, more precisely, defines such a soul?

One clue might lie in the words of Robert Henri, writing in *The Art Spirit:* "The reason so many artists have lived to great age and have been so young at great age is that to such extent they have lived living, whereas most people live dying."

When we live living we live affirmatively. Undeterred by whatever life may throw at us, we display a bias for living – in contrast to many fearful people who, consciously or not, display a bias for dying. People who live living generally have a stronger sense of calling than others. They see what they do as "the right thing."

How do we know what we are called to do? How do we know what is right for us? The answer is that we can feel it in our bones. It resonates at our core and perpetually enlivens us. We stay younger longer, in mind and body.

Seeing our place in the world "rightly" spurs us to take commensurately right actions, which make our lives all the more open, vital, and unified. In the evolved, transparent person the inner and outer selves match up. The spirit is true, and so the self that meets the world is consequently true. The goal in life is to align these inner and outer selves so that people can look clearly into your soul and see a faithful reflection beneath of what they observe on the surface. People can see into you because you are not afraid to have them look. Openness in this case is not vulnerability. It is a form of wisdom because the honest man has nothing to hide. He is free of guile, and therefore free of guilt.

### What is is

A prerequisite to gaining wisdom is the acknowledgement of things as they really are, not as we wish them to be. When we see things clearly we begin to take control of our lives. Nathaniel Branden explains this idea in his book, T*aking Responsibility: Self-Reliance and the Accountable Life:*

> Intellectual sovereignty, self-reliance, and self-responsibility are rooted in a firm sense of reality. This means a deep respect for facts. What is is. Things are what they are. Truth is not obliterated by the refusal to see it. Facts are not annihilated by the pretense that they do not exist...We must grasp and respect the distinction between the real and the unreal, between facts, on the one hand, and wishes, hopes, fears, and fantasies on the other.

In my life, I have felt disappointment in some other people, and some have doubtless felt the same in me. Looking back, the fault has been just as much mine as theirs. I have been either too exacting, too wishful, or simply too naive when it came to the behavior of certain other people. Eventually, I began to acknowledge situations, other people, and myself as they and I really were. Becoming more realistic in my appraisal of others forced me to understand that I had to be the same way with myself. From that new premise I was able to act with more precision in my relationships. More precision resulted in fewer but better relationships. Those better relationships have helped hone my awareness of reality – of what is, as opposed to what is not.

### Don't Hope; Will

People who favor the unreal over "what is" can fall into the habit of denial. As a consequence, they often have a hard time fulfilling their ambitions. They become mired in delusion, captive to wishful thinking, and often frustrated by a life that does not conform to expectation. They experience undue disappointment, and, in extreme cases, cast themselves as chronic victims.

Idealism is not a bad thing, but for it to assume heft it must be clear in conception and pragmatic in action.

"Hope" was a word I used to use often. While it is such a positive-sounding word, an excess of hope can represent a psychological trap. Hoping that things will turn out a certain way rarely makes them so. Prefacing a sentence with the words "I hope" belies an underlying lack of confidence in oneself and an expectation that disappointment might result. (It also signals a plea for divine intervention.) Otherwise, why hope to begin with?

If you really seek a certain result then get into the habit of saying, "I want," "I expect," or, "I will," and follow up what you say with considered action. When we take our lives to the world with clear intentions we diminish fear and worry. We become more responsible for the outcomes we seek. We stop wishing for certain results and start creating them.

## We are Our Energy

A person is the product of his health. A person's health is the product of how easily energy flows through his body, mind, and soul. A healthy existence is about getting in touch with your energy and making it work for, not against, you. A good and happy life exudes positive energy and palpable grace.

A good life is open, bountiful, expansive. It welcomes things in, absorbs their essence, and graciously and gently releases them back out to the stream of life. It enhances what it touches. A good life does not get attached to things. It does not hoard, nor does it skimp. It avoids sentimentality and obsession. It does not resist when it does not understand. Consequently, it does not constrict flow and create energy blockages. Rather, it overcomes any resistance encountered through sustained, sincere, and graceful effort that dissolves obstacles or deftly maneuvers around them.

Some years back, I found out firsthand how dangerous stagnation can be. My feeling thwarted in my personal and professional lives generated an inner frustration and resentment, which ultimately contributed, I now believe, to a diagnosis of cancer in the fall of 1999. In metaphysical terms my energy was blocked. My life was dammed up, my ambitions stymied. I was unable to express myself as fully as I needed to and was inept at channeling my energies in healthier directions.

Energy never goes away. It migrates from one place to another or assumes a different form, whether that's inside our bodies or in the environment around us. I believe that the blocked psychic energy in my life contributed to a sizeable cancerous mass that appeared in my neck. In retrospect, that tumor was a blessing, a forceful sign that it was time for me to change my life or risk more dire consequences.

### Wholeness Equals Health

After I was diagnosed with Non Hodgkin's Lymphoma, I resolved to play a game with myself. I thought of my immune system as a "bank" into which I could make daily deposits. Happy thoughts and positive, kindly actions would be "deposits," or "credits." Negative thinking, emotions, and actions would amount to "withdrawals."

The bottom line on our health is that it is only as strong as our immune system. How readily we handle the shocks and minor assaults of daily existence determines how our health plays out in the long run. We should, therefore, strive to make daily deposits in our immune banks and discipline ourselves to limit the withdrawals.

My prior indebtedness took a very tangible form. But I was lucky; I got a second chance. The tumor turned out to be largely self-contained, allowing a skilled surgeon to remove it from my body, even though it was sitting atop my carotid artery.

That left me with a much smaller, slower-growing tumor in my abdomen. Malignant in nature yet benign in size, it is something I have been carrying with me for the past five years. I try to

# THE GROUND OF PERSONAL MASTERY

think of this tumor as important "company," something that reminds me that I must keep making frequent deposits in my immunity bank in an effort to keep paying down whatever debts I had previously incurred.

### Philosophy is the Way

The way to transmute our energy from bad to good, from negative to positive, is through philosophy. I am not speaking so much about the study of philosophy, but rather the living of a philosophic life. Such an existence entails an abiding love of knowledge, a bias to openness, and a consequent pursuit of truthful awareness. The philosophic person is an engaged, intentional being. He is both pragmatist and seeker. He is awake, and he is strong enough so that his psychological defenses are down. A kindly courage is his constant companion.

What then exactly is a philosophic life?

It is one that balances awareness with practice. It is about getting into the game by consciously living such qualities as openness, honesty, and love. If you can do that with consistent effort and sincerity you begin to unshackle yourself from the inherent randomness of life. "To win true freedom you must be a slave to philosophy," wrote Epicurus. Adds Seneca, "A person who surrenders and subjects himself to her (philosophy) doesn't have his application deferred from day to day; he's emancipated on the spot, the very service of philosophy being freedom."

A person lives philosophically and gains liberation not simply through study but by actively investing what he learns in his life. If his effort is right and true then his life will assume a similar cast. It will be balanced, well-made, and whole, not to mention obvious to all. Others will heed his example, not because he seeks to instruct but because they choose to observe.

CHAPTER TWO

# THE NATURE OF BELIEF

### Become Mentally Fit

In recent years we have heard much about obesity in America. Less obvious, but equally epidemic, is the country's mental flabbiness. Poor language skills, a woeful inability to write, and a general dearth of critical thinking are some of the earmarks of a society that is mentally out of shape.

The information society in which we live is a faux knowledge society. The devaluation of knowledge and loss of context is the result of living in a society awash in information, much of it of dubious worth. A surfeit of data pumped out by a proliferating array of media has flooded our mental filters. No matter the subject, we now have the ability to quickly select from a wealth of "facts" that often do little more than reinforce what we already think.

We stand at a pivotal point in world history when the United States is investing considerable blood and treasure to help instill democratic ideals in parts of the world that have traditionally been hostile to such values. Yet does American democracy, itself, risk imploding by dint of our intellectual sloth; for our failure to grasp that the unfiltered flow of information can be just as toxic as raw sewage running through the streets?

One way out of this morass is for individuals to commit to getting their minds in shape. We should read more widely, force ourselves out of our respective intellectual comfort zones more often, and actively entertain those views that differ from ours. In any discussion favor facts, reason, and logic over opinions. The latter are freely expended because they have been freely acquired, and as the adage goes, "You get what you pay for." Bluster, in ample supply these days in the public square, often is a handy mask for ignorance and insecurity.

### Knowledge is Goodness

A respect for knowledge is a noble thing for a variety of reasons. Beyond encouraging civility in the larger society, it puts the individual citizen on the path to wisdom. Wisdom cultivates a calm, contented mind. "No one can lead a happy life, or even one that is bearable, without the pursuit of wisdom," writes Seneca. "And it is the perfection of wisdom that makes for the happy life."

The pursuit of wisdom gives us the courage to consider divergent ideas. It opens our minds and reduces our fear of contrary voices and unpleasant facts. Through open-mindedness we gain not simply an awareness of our purpose in the world, but an appreciation, too, of why others are here. By cultivating respect and empathy – for oneself as well as for others – we gain goodness. When we close ourselves off from knowledge we do the reverse, hardening our hearts and minds to our neighbor's lot.

# THE NATURE OF BELIEF

The least virtuous of men tend to be the most self-regarding. They are in love with themselves and their ideas to the exclusion of virtually all others. It is no coincidence that Osama bin Laden has closed his mind to any thought other than his own dogma or that Kim Jung Il has sealed off his country from the rest of the world. And it is consequently no surprise that the former would exult over skyscrapers being transformed into crematoria, or the latter would allow millions of his countrymen to starve while he obsessively pursued nuclear arms. In their absolute refusal to consider the views and humanity of others, bin Laden and Jung Il reveal the depths of their ignorance.

## Goodness is a Competitive Advantage

The pursuit of knowledge not only rouses our awareness of virtue. It encourages its practice.

Practicing virtue informs our lives with a sense of fairness. We get into the habit of being open and honest in our dealings. We do not fear being taken advantage of because we know that good is a positive force which trumps lesser motives. "Moral qualities are not ineffective things," writes Haridas Chaudhuri in *The Essence of Spiritual Philosophy*. "They are not simply our mental ideas. They are objective forces in life and nature."

Chaudhuri and other eastern thinkers believe that goodness creates favorable karma, which is to be distinguished from fate. Karma isn't something that just happens to us. Through our conduct we create it, and thereby own it. By being our ideas we become agents of our respective destinies and, accordingly, guide our lives. Thus, goodness is more than simply its own reward. It's a tangible way of living that amounts to a competitive advantage. Here, more specifically, is why:

*It feels good.* A sense of goodness imparts a prevailing positive thrust to a person's life. It makes the practitioner, himself, feel good because being for something is easier – and happier – than being against it. "A good character is the only guarantee of everlasting, carefree happiness," writes Seneca. Note his use of the word 'carefree.' When a person is in favor of something he tends to be in the flow of life and less prey to its frictive forces. When he opposes things he typically resists that flow. Fighting the current wears him down. He becomes *careworn*.

*Virtue travels lightly.* By practicing goodness we shed unwanted feelings, notably our doubts, fears, and resentments. That frees us to practice virtuous conduct all the more.

*People prefer to deal with good people.* Transactions between sincere, well-intentioned people are typically smoother and more pleasurable. They are fairer and more profitable for all concerned. Goodness attracts the right allies – people who respect you and wish to share their energy with yours. They sense that associating with you will reinforce right conduct in their own lives.

## Work on Yourself, Not Others

After working for nearly 30 years as a professional journalist, I moved to the woods of upstate New York to do other things. One of those pursuits was being a personal coach. Doing that seemed

## THE NATURE OF BELIEF

a natural choice as I felt, given my life experience, I could guide and motivate others. Wishing to share my knowledge, I resolved to quietly hang out my shingle and let potential clients find me.

I was comfortable with this arrangement because while I believe I have some worthy insights to offer, I also know that you cannot tell others what to do. The best a person can do is keep working on himself – strive to live right, every day. If he does that then he will gain a sufficient following.

Many people are inclined to work on others, not themselves. It is easier to judge, criticize, and control others because it spares us the hard and often painful work of turning an exacting eye on ourselves. But that just compounds our problems. As Haridas Chaudhuri notes, "When you hammer too much upon sinfulness and crime you may become sinful."

But when you quietly work on yourself, you, typically, head in the opposite direction – toward virtue. Notice how people who refrain from judging others often project serenity and a dignified sense of limit. They know their bounds. Conversely, there are few people more undignified and intrusive than those who preach one thing and do another. The word "preach," here, is fitting because a number of such examples that come to mind involve various religious leaders who have preached the good word while engaging in questionable deeds. Another relevant case might be that of the former Secretary of Education, William Bennett, who has made a career out of all but trademarking the term "virtue," while simultaneously indulging a heavy gambling habit.

It's a good idea to question the instructions of others when they are uttered with a moral certainty, which can be a poor proxy for moral *clarity*. In a similar vein, we might also question some of society's time-honored directives. These would include:

*"Duty" is often a ruse perpetrated by those in power to keep the individual in line, enlist him to perform dangerous or unpleasant tasks, and preserve the status quo.* By making the individual feel beholden to some "higher" calling, society cultivates his latent sense of guilt and controls him.

If you always feel a duty to others you will never serve and complete yourself. A person's first duty is to himself. It is to the task of becoming as thoughtful, artful, courageous, and soulful as he can possibly become. If he accomplishes this task then he will discharge his true obligations to others.

The ideal community is one peopled by as many skilled practitioners of as many crafts, trades, and professions as possible. People who have been freed to do what they do best create the strongest social glue. They act voluntarily and in concert with their peers.

One should beware of the overly duty-bound man who trumpets his cause, or, worse, projects his grand, "heroic" yearnings onto others. These people often anoint themselves as "martyrs," forever willing, they claim, to "sacrifice" for the rest of us because we are selfishly fixated on our own petty desires. (Hitler, it should be noted, was one of the sternest critics of personal happiness.) Ultimately, though, he sacrifices others to his cause. He does so to ensure his own preservation. Some of the cruelest acts of modern times have been perpetrated under the guise of exalted common cause by the likes of Lenin, Stalin, Hitler, Mao, and, more recently,

# THE NATURE OF BELIEF

Pol Pot, Hussein, and Bin Laden. These men are not the saviors they imagine themselves to be, but damaged, albeit clever, men who struggle to survive as self-contained and accountable individuals. The martyr may claim to love humanity but not human beings, toward whom he freely exhibits the greatest contempt.

As the philosopher, Eric Hoffer, notes in *The True Believer: Thoughts on the Nature of Mass Movements*:

> The fiercest fanatics are often selfish people who were forced, by innate shortcomings or external circumstances, to lose faith in their own selves. They separate the excellent instrument of their selfishness from their ineffectual selves and attach it to the service of some holy cause. And though it be a faith of love and humility they adopt, they can be neither loving nor humble.

*Guilt is the martyr's currency.* We spend too much of our lives – and emotional capital – doing what others have coerced us into believing we should do. While we often seek to discharge duties and fulfill roles as laid out by family, society, or institutions, the expectations that matter most are those we develop for ourselves. The best way not to disappoint others is to not disappoint ourselves.

Many of us have this ill-defined feeling that we "should" be doing something, or that we are not doing enough. But this struggle to conform to others' expectations often results in capitulation to their dictates. This diverts us from fulfilling our own ambitions.

When people expunge this vague and gnawing sense of obligation from their lives they take the first step toward transforming themselves from helpless and guilt-driven to self-directed and responsible. If you begin each day with a short list of the things you intend to get done and consciously will yourself to do them then you will accomplish much in life, while also understanding that you "owe" no one other than yourself.

The chief aim of guilt is to mentally paralyze us and coax us into surrendering our sense of purpose to others. The theft of the energy of the hard-working populace by an "elite" few is the hallmark of the unevolved community. It is sadly how too many businesses, societies, and even institutions of higher learning are still "governed" in today's world.

*"Sin" is a form of control.* Sin flows from guilt. It trafficks mainly in negatives and relies on arbitrary authority. The Ten Commandments, which are mainly about things we should *not* do, also suggest something ordered from on high. Moses, after all, brought them down from the mountaintop.

Note that history has proven the top-down, "command" economies and political systems that arose behind the Iron Curtain to be bloody and ruinous failures. Toilet paper shortages and long lines for rotting fruit were among the more benign consequences of such illegitimate governance.

The truth is that each of us has the potential to know himself the best. Therefore, shouldn't each of us strive to be the arbiter of his own actions? That is the natural way. Moreover, aren't we better off advising people to tell the truth as opposed to instructing them not to lie? After all, when most of us get up in the morning we are inclined to do certain things. We don't set out not to do them.

Our default instinct, therefore, should be "towards yes," as Nathaniel Branden puts it, in *Taking Responsibility: Self-Reliance and the Accountable Life.* Doing so, he tells us, gives our lives a loving bias. "If we love someone, it seems natural to want to respond affirmatively to his or her desires, although obviously it is not always possible to do so," Branden writes. "But one of the ways love is expressed is through the bias being on the side of yes."

*Honor is a noble-sounding word that often assumes – falsely – iconic status.* It sits there leadenly, as inert as a monument, commanding the blind devotion of one generation after another. Wiser heads, however, understand the limiting nature of "honor." Consider Aristotle's shrewd take on the subject: "People seem to seek honor in order to convince themselves of their own goodness."

Honor can become a stick with which to herd, and even beat, people into submission. We are told that we should cloak ourselves in honor; we should bring honor to one's family or country. That kind of phrasing is redolent of the Mafia or the Nazi Party, among the most dishonorable of known enterprises. Once you join one of these "blood honor" societies you are committed for life. The only way out is through death. The only way to stay in is to kill.

Honor carries more weight – and less baggage – as a verb. It assumes energy – and connotes giving rather than receiving. When a person honors his mate, his family, his friends he bestows a mindful respect on others, rather than having a vague sense of guilt-inducing obligation forced upon him. Honor in this active sense gives a man will and autonomy. He acts from his own beliefs, his own consciousness. He chooses his own course rather than passively assuming directives from others. He decides for himself what is important – what things he will, in fact, honor.

### Re-evaluate Faith

Words like duty, guilt, honor, and sin belong to the vocabulary of the 20th century, an era during which more people died due to more isms than in any previous era of human history. With a new century upon us, we are overdue for a major reevaluation of many of our beliefs and the institutions that reinforce them. We are already starting to see this process unfold. Its hallmarks are:

- *Less hierarchy and rigidity in human organization.* Enhanced collaboration and flexibility.

- *A greater emphasis on the exercise of free will and democratic principles.*

- *A sharper questioning of institutional behavior and institutional ways of thinking.*

- *The rejection of ideology in favor of philosophy.* The latter entails a love of knowledge. The former profits from man's ignorance and credulity.

Turning the above ideas into reality entails a renewed belief in the worth and wisdom of the individual. That means rejecting the collective – *not* the community – which often amounts to nothing more than the individual abdicating will and identity to the mob.

**God is in the Details**

Part of this effort requires rethinking the nature of God.

God exists to rouse the wonder in man, not to demand his obedience and remind him of his sinfulness. He is omnipresent in our lives, not omnipotent. He does not judge. The man who understands God's true nature becomes free to live in a respectful, conscientious manner. He can stop looking over his shoulder, wondering how the "authorities," religious and otherwise, will view his behavior. He knows whatever spiritual guidance he needs is staring him right in the face.

When I walk in the woods daily around my house and see the artistry of nature in the simplest things – dead leaves, rotting stumps, the drift of a stream over rocks – I ask myself, two questions. First, how can God not be here? Second, if God is in the details, as he surely is in nature, then how can he be anything but a subtle force who has elicited – not commanded – my respect? Isn't he simply an animating force present in all things alongside man, not looming over him as the proverbial "Almighty?"

The major religions are in danger of becoming relics. Represented by institutions that are in decline, they desperately seek to re-exert influence over their respective "flocks" in order to perpetuate themselves and preserve their eroding power. The sex abuse scandal and subsequent stonewalling that recently engulfed the Catholic Church is no historical accident. Neither is the failure of mainstream Islam – which has presided over seven centuries of social and political regression – to speak out forcefully against the terrorists who corrupt its message.

### Practice Makes Possible

The way back from the failure of faith, which has only produced diminishing returns for more and more people, is to untangle – liberate – spirituality from religion. Doing so asks more of the individual. He must know his own mind. He must know what he believes, not what others have told him to believe. That requires mental discipline and maturity.

Mental discipline is a vital prerequisite to spiritual growth. Books on eastern philosophy commonly note its absence through various metaphors such as "tigers in need of taming," or, more sobering, "chattering monkeys jumping up and down at open windows." These same books, similarly, stress how essential it is to develop mental discipline. Hence the emphasis in these religions on meditation as a means of controlling and directing our faculties. As we rein in our thoughts and reclaim their ownership, we begin to grasp the task we have assumed. Keeping the mind autonomous, calm, and clear requires a spiritual bent, which, in turn, relies on mental discipline? How do we impose that?

We do it through the "practices" we take on, whether they are meditation, prayer, writing, reading, work, raising children, or pursuing a hobby, pastime, or sport. It is through mindful devotion to our pursuits, large and small, that we begin building the necessary mental strength to take the next vital step, doing our "soul work."

## Soul Work Regulates the Self

By doing one's soul work, or "growing one's soul," I mean engaging in the honest labor that frees the self to evolve toward becoming a better, kinder, stronger, truer, more aware, more capable, more independent, and more artful human being. This is an essential mission of life, and we begin to fulfill it when we move out from under the shadow of others' rules and into the light of self-regulation. It is about putting yourself in a position where no one tells you what to do – and vice versa – because you have gained a clear and proper sense of what to do. You are on the right path.

A self-regulated life creates the firm psychological ground of happiness. "People who lead a satisfying life, who are in tune with their past and their future – in short, people whom we would call 'happy' – are generally individuals who have lived their lives according to rules they themselves created," writes Mihaly Csikszentmihalyi in *Flow: The Psychology of Optimal Experience:*

> They eat according to their own schedules, sleep when they are sleepy, work because they enjoy doing it, choose their friends and relationships for good reasons. They understand their motives and their limitations. They have carved out a small freedom of choice.

In sum, happy (self-regulated) people live beyond the reach of arbitrary rules, yet they invariably respect the rights of others.

## Self-Regulation Liberates

Self-regulation is about opening up and letting go. It is about stepping into an open and sunny place, where there is no hiding, and where energy abounds. It's about expanding your senses as wide as possible to draw in experience as fully as possible. Do that and a consequent bounty will flow your way.

Self-regulation is a form of openness because it comes from a fearless place. Many people actively seek out structure, routine, and authority because freedom scares them. But the self-regulated person welcomes his freedom. He does not fear its consequences because he knows that his actions are correct.

Self-regulation dissolves the oppositional nature of existence that puts us in conflict with one another and negates our common energy. It creates unity in the form of a single point where all facets of life merge and resolve themselves peacefully. When we do our soul work we do not just find harmony; we create it. Right actions lead to right results. Right results reinforce right living.

Practicing self-regulation is as straightforward as it is liberating. It is about learning to act mindfully in all things. As we do our soul work we build on the inside. We can then begin to dismantle the false ego structures we have fabricated on the outside. We can start to shed our airs and fears because our work on the inside strengthens us all the more. Think of it as shoveling snow off the roof. As we lift that external weight, the stress on the structure beneath lessens. Each element – the building action we take on the inside, and the lightening action we take on the outside – reinforces the other. Progress becomes progressively easier.

## THE NATURE OF BELIEF

The result is the strong person who is imbued with feeling. He is the true person; well put together and possessed of a structural integrity. He is self-contained; a person of firmness, conviction, and calm.

CHAPTER THREE

# THE SELF IN ACTION

**Develop an 'Immunity to Fear'**

To live wisely is to live boldly.

Living wisely requires summoning the courage to script your own life, no matter what convention might dictate or what others might think. But once a person decides to do so he lives boldly, or as Seneca puts it, "There is nothing the wise man does reluctantly." In fact, Seneca adds, he develops "an immunity to fear for which he can thank his own efforts." The wise man does what he has to do, no matter the consequences, no matter the opinion of others – because he knows he must.

Taking decisive action clarifies thought and reinforces courage. When we stop making halfhearted gestures we stop settling for half measures. Montaigne writes about "leaping audacity's barriers" in order to establish "noble means for a noble end." In other words, honest effort burns away self-doubt.

We begin to align our actions with our goals by fully applying our interior assets to effect good and meaningful results in the world. When we wisely invest our intellectual and emotional capital it produces spiritual riches for us and an attendant bounty for those we meet along the way.

### Clear Action Builds Confidence

It is important to rely on yourself for as many things as you possibly can. Teach yourself to cook simply but with flair; eat well, exercise right, get comfortable with tools, and learn how to manage your money. Read widely and learn to think critically. Always be ready to try new things and consider unorthodox points of view.

Be aware that the conventional wisdom is usually wrong and that the great steps forward are made incrementally by fearless, free-thinking, and spirited individuals who are prepared to accept the ridicule that others may heap on them.

"Venerate your faculty of judgment," writes Marcus Aurelius. "For nothing is so conducive to elevation of mind as to be able to examine methodically and truthfully everything that presents itself in life.

"In all that you undertake, you must look on things and act in such a way that at the same time you ensure that the duties imposed on you by circumstances are accomplished and your powers of thought are fully exercised, and that the self-confidence which arises from a proper understanding of each particular thing is maintained with discretion, but without concealment."

Confidence – borne of, and nurtured by, well-considered action – will energize your life. Once you commit to the "proper understanding of each particular thing" you have set out on the path to living a full, confident, and interesting life.

# THE SELF IN ACTION

## Lean Into Life

The interesting life displays a bias to experiment. When a person leans into life it opens him up all the more to its possibilities. He projects into living, and so encounters experience more readily. It's like resolving to jump into a 60-degree ocean. You know you are in for a shock, but you also know that taking the plunge will enliven you. Coming out of the water you'll feel ten years younger.

The open person, facing life squarely, is a realist in the best and truest sense of the word. He acknowledges the reality of the world (the coldness of the water.) Still, he welcomes it because he knows it will invigorate him.

The realist, therefore, is the true optimist because, by taking action, he comes to know what is possible and what is not. He is prepared to find a way to fulfillment, no matter the obstacles.

The realist is what the psychologist Abraham Maslow would call the "self-actualizing" person. This is the person who is motivated to live a whole, integrated life. He must do so; he has no choice because he feels the need to set a true course in life, and he cannot deny that urge. It is his reason for being. He does not delude himself about what he can achieve, yet he also knows he cannot turn back. So he knows the stakes, and he sees the hurdles before him. When life is laid out this way in front of you, you see it clearly and courageously. Good things become possible.

## Trust Creates Opportunity

People who are open to experience tend to be trusting people. Because they have learned how to trust their own instincts, they are better disposed to trust others. They are more prepared, for example, to do deals with a handshake because they have developed a sense for what feels right between people.

Increasingly in my life, I have sought and been prepared to do business with people because on first meeting them I simply liked and trusted them. And if I liked them then they were more apt to be not just honest, but skilled and professional as well. I was prepared to buy my last house within minutes of first seeing it from the street at dusk on a cold November day because the situation felt right for me, and I trusted my real estate agent.

I was prepared to buy my latest car, a secondhand Jeep, after a five-minute phone call with the dealer. A trip out to see him – he picked me up at the train station – followed by a short test drive and a handshake on a no-haggle price sealed the deal.

I sensed in these purchases not just good deals, but good transactions as they presented opportunities to avail myself of the better side of human nature. Open people generally know what they want because their bias to experience sharpens their instincts when it comes to knowing what is fair, honest, and mutually beneficial. They have a good feel for human nature. They also understand that greed or coercion in the pursuit of any deal only drives it further from reach.

## Be Playful

Openness equates with innocence and youthfulness of spirit. (It is childlike, not childish.) When we are open we stay young and flexible of mind. Playfulness is a positive attribute. Cultivate a mirthful spirit and you will summon good cheer into your life.

THE SELF IN ACTION

Humorless people are closed people, as laughter, by definition, is an expansive act. Closed people age prematurely. Their cheerlessness blocks them from drawing positive energy from life, as they focus on survival, not living. They do not realize that the energy they so desperately seek to hoard is dissipating all the time. Conversely, when we relax and open ourselves to experience we readily draw energy to us. We gain the life force itself.

**Make Your Interest Genuine**

Life is about taking care of business, today. Deal with what's in front of you. See to your commitments on a daily basis. Boil life down to a few essential activities that suit you, are a part of who you are, and that you really care about. In other words, ask yourself, "Who am I, and how do I go about actualizing my identity, not just in my life but in my day?" Days well spent build into a life well lived.

A person should be able to count the meaningful roles he plays in life on one hand and strive to fulfill each of them daily. When I consider who I really am I can boil the list down to the following: father, friend, writer/ coach, and athlete. That's pretty much it. By enacting these few well-considered roles I can invest enough energy in each to hopefully do them well and do them justice.

If you care about something you will focus on it and stand a better chance of doing it well. And doing things well reinforces a sense of caring. As Bertrand Russell notes in *The Conquest of Happiness,* "All serious success in work depends upon some genuine interest in the material with which the work is concerned." When you care, even the most mundane of tasks assume meaning and provide satisfaction. In recent years, as I became more committed to giving my thoughts voice in the form of this book, I became more mindful of keeping a tidier house and a stricter schedule. These tasks did not amount to irrelevant chores but appropriate preparations for my taking the main job, writing, more seriously.

**Hard Work Makes Life Easy**

The ability to focus daily on a few core tasks and fulfill them builds the confidence necessary to tackle larger, more difficult problems as they arise. This, at the end of the day, is what separates the people who rise in life from those who do not. The confidence we gain from completing even simple jobs effectively girds us for life's bigger challenges.

The "easy way out" is called that for good reason. It is the easy way out not just of specific tasks, but of life itself. The easy way translates as avoidance and denial. It is not facing up to what needs doing. It is choosing those things that negate our energies over those that nourish them.

The antidote to the easy thing is the right thing. If you get in the habit of doing the right thing then in time it becomes the genuinely easy thing. We simply know what we must do, and that knowledge strengthens our will to accomplish it. How then do you identify the right thing? The right thing happens when we take actions that move us forward. Right actions test us and make us stronger, healthier, more *accomplished* human beings. The right thing is not just the responsible thing, but the fulfilling thing.

# THE SELF IN ACTION

We live in a fat culture, with some 60% of the adult population overweight. Such a society favors those things that ease life. But if we take the easy way too often then soon enough we discover that life is hard. The "good life" to which we aspire can, in fact, be bad for our health.

It is no mere coincidence that a fat culture reveres the television, enshrining this medium for passive entertainment at the center of the so-called "family room." (In fact, the TV has even burrowed its way to the nucleus of what we now call the "home entertainment center.") It's a good idea to relegate the TV to the periphery of the house, just as other "easy" things should be consigned to the margins of a life. I am not talking about banishing the television, but putting it in its appropriate place, where it can be used at the viewer's discretion and not its dictate. (In most things, moderation is a typically more effective prescription than abstinence.) Such action opens and reclaims the fruitful center of life. It clears a space for sharper thought, better actions, and good living in earnest.

**Get Into the Arena**

If you pull back from such distractions as television and the various "conveniences" that often end up complicating our days, you prepare yourself to engage fully with life. You become less distracted and more open to experience. I noticed this in my younger son who, as he neared the end of high school, gave up playing video games. By the time he got to college he was ready to dive into his major, Biology, and join the crew team. This latter commitment requires that he rise three days a week at 6 A.M.

## TRUE SPIRIT, TRUE SELF

What matters is not how you play the game, but simply getting into the game. Teddy Roosevelt called that "being in the arena," and here is how he described it:

> It is not the critic who counts, not the man who points out how the strong man stumbles or where the doer of deeds could have done them better. The credit belongs to the man who is actually in the arena, whose face is marred by dust and sweat and blood, who strives valiantly, who errs and comes up short again and again because there is no effort without error and shortcomings, who knows the great devotion, who spends himself in a worthy cause.

The deeper message behind Roosevelt's exhortation is clear:

*Be an actor, not an observer or critic.* Each of us is here to make an active contribution to the world that is uniquely ours. If you live vicariously or passively you will never make that contribution. The privilege will pass to others.

*Do not fear failure.* It is typically a better teacher than success because it gets our attention. Success, as often as not, can be delusory by causing us to mistake luck for talent.

*When success comes keep it in perspective.* Allow it to humble you, and it will recur to you. Gloat over it, and it will desert you. You have to keep going. Keep pushing forward to the next small triumph, honestly pursued, and, therefore, honestly gained.

# THE SELF IN ACTION

*Life is about enduring.* Endurance at its core is not grand, nor heroic; it is incremental. Endurance is effort applied honestly and sincerely, daily. Live each day as if it is your last. Think of it as the day that "rounds out" your life, as Seneca puts it. The rounded out life, like a balanced wheel, turns true and easy.

## Make Harmony Your Ruling Power

Stepping into the arena actually softens the harshness of life because we are now – courageously – engaged with it, not living estranged from it. We take responsibility for the course we set because we have willingly chosen it. Life will then open itself to us. Life becomes fruitful and comprehensible when we wade right in, undefended, and partake of it for better or worse. Taking action conquers doubt and fear. It reinforces awareness.

The happiest people in life are the most fearless and the most conscious. They are not afraid to stare reality in the eye, indeed to make friends with it. They are not afraid to consider their own limitations and push against them. They work with what they have, not with what they wish they had.

"To set your mind against anything that comes to pass is to set yourself apart from nature," wrote Marcus Aurelius. In other words, when we stop "setting our minds" against "what is" and acknowledge the facts before us we stop resisting life. We start going with it. We work with our reality, or as Marcus Aurelius goes on to say: "When the ruling power within us is harmony with nature, it confronts what comes to pass in such a way that it always adapts itself with ease to what is practicable and what is granted for it."

## TRUE SPIRIT, TRUE SELF

### Passion Invites Action

The noted American painted and art teacher, Robert Henri, writes in his classic, *The Art Spirit*:

> There are two classes of human beings. One has ideas, which it believes in fully, perhaps, but modifies to bring about "success." The other class has ideas which it believes in and must carry out absolutely; success or no success. The first class has a tremendous majority, and they are all slaves. The second class are the only free people in the world.

If you are passionate and "absolute," as Henri describes it, then you will develop a bias toward action. Taking action creates experience, which, in turn, raises awareness. You forge a *virtuous circle of identity*, which can be described as follows:

- Passion (belief) triggers action.
- Action creates experience.
- Experience cultivates awareness.
- Awareness stokes passion.

The aware man is by definition a man who is open to happiness because he is willing – unafraid – to examine himself and his world. He wants to understand and experience as much as possible. True happiness is impossible without a healthy amount of awareness because awareness forms the ground for psychological integrity (which translates as honesty out in the world) and there can be no such thing as a dishonest happiness. If we cannot be

# THE SELF IN ACTION

honest with ourselves then we cannot be honest with others, and our quest for happiness breaks down.

Any addictive, excessive, delusional, avoidant, or compulsive behavior, conversely, is ultimately dishonest and, therefore, inauthentic. It is at root unhappy action. It is a form of forgetting and thus, by definition, diminishes awareness and curiosity. (It is also a form of "absolute" behavior in the negative sense.) The more people act this way, the more they seek oblivion and removal from awareness. And the more they do that, the more they distance themselves from the prospect of happiness.

### Love the Battle

It is important to remember that facing reality is not easy. Life bangs up all of us. Disappointment, and tragedy even, is simply the price of admission to life. In fact, when we deny disappointment we compound regret.

On the other hand, disappointment acknowledged opens our eyes. When we stand our ground and take life's hits we grow stronger and wiser, meaning we better position ourselves to sustain or sidestep future blows. If you get in the habit of ducking all your life then you will never learn – and you will grow increasingly more afraid. The bill will one day come due with serious interest. You will become paralyzed by fear, unable to take action.

People who simply orient by their appetites, habits, and fears eventually pay a price down the road, for no one can simply skid through life. If you are once burned, resist the impulse to be twice shy. Take the time to go into yourself, heal, and consider. When you take stock this way you stand a better chance of coming out

## TRUE SPIRIT, TRUE SELF

the other side emboldened yet appropriately humble – and ready again to join the fray. How then does one practice this sort of right and courageous effort? By adopting a mindset that "loves the battle," in the words of Jim Loehr, the author of *The Mental Game: Winning at Pressure Tennis*.

Loehr is a sports psychologist who has worked with many top-ranked professional tennis players as well as other elite athletes. One quality he sees in great tennis players is an ability to quickly and calmly walk away from errors and focus on the next point. They quickly consign their mistakes to where they belong, the past. Yes, these champions want to win, but, more important, they understand that the real rewards arise from engaging wholeheartedly and positively in the competitive process, which occurs in the present. And that means playing with commitment and concentration – not with an eye on the scoreboard, or with the mind pondering what might have been.

In contrast, many of us are more interested in results or in looking good. We care less for the pursuit than for the prize or prestige because if we can we'd just as soon avoid putting in the hard work that yields a full and meaningful result.

The question then becomes: How can we exalt process to make it more joyful, to make it more of a habit? Loehr's advice is to focus on what he labels "mastery goals," as opposed to "outcome goals." He explains the distinction this way:

> Mastery goals (often referred to as performance goals) deal with effort, learning, competence and improvement; outcome goals deal with end results, final outcomes, and ulti-

mate ends. Examples of mastery goals are learning to give 100 percent, learning to get more depth and spin on your second serve, learning to be more positive and aggressive during play. Examples of outcome goals are winning a specific game, match, or tournament. Mastery goals enable you to carve out a sense of success even when you lose. Finding success in a losing effort helps prevent feelings of helplessness. You can't directly control winning, but you can always control your effort, attitude, sense of fight, and commitment to learning.

### Learn from the Challenge

How, more precisely, can we learn to love the battle? Here are some thoughts on that:

*Go to the ball.* On the tennis court there is a simple maxim, which says, "Go to the Ball." Translation: Simply do what needs doing. In tennis, that means doing what it takes to get to the ball before it bounces a second time. If you don't do that then you lose the point. In life, that means living directly. Take care of today what needs taking care of today.

"Always run by the shortest route; and the shortest is that which follows nature, and leads us to say and do everything in the soundest fashion," counsels Marcus Aurelius.

He is referring to the need to inform our actions with an economy that mimics nature and an intentionality that is fully conscious and, therefore, quintessentially human. When we focus and direct our energy this way we get the most out of it.

## TRUE SPIRIT, TRUE SELF

*Burn yourself up.* Be conscious of throwing yourself fully into those things you do. Offering complete effort draws down your batteries as completely as possible, thereby allowing you to recharge them all the more fully and efficiently. I find it hardly surprising that my best nights of sleep follow days filled with vigorous excersise. Focusing and expending energy in the right way and on the right tasks doesn't weaken us. It does the opposite. It deepens our reserves and makes us stronger.

*Run to daylight.* Part of life is inevitably finding obstacles strewn in our path. This is often not intentional, but the result is the same, confusion and needless worry. The antidote is to be on the lookout for openings in our lives which create a way out and through to situations that offer clarity and the freer flow of energy. When we run into walls or dead ends they are not trying to stop us; they are simply trying to send us in new, more hopeful directions. (In other words, they are there for good reason.)

A few years ago, I woke up one morning and decided that I needed to move from a suburb near Boston to a town in the Adirondack Mountains. I cannot rationally explain this decision, other than to say that the Adirondacks was an area to which I had maintained a connection of sorts for much of my life. Within two weeks I was looking at houses in the area, and a month later I had found something to buy. That was the easy part.

I was only able to afford the purchase by taking a calculated risk. I borrowed against the equity in my existing house. That meant that for more than a year, until I sold my first house and actually made the move, I would be carrying a considerable

## THE SELF IN ACTION

amount of debt. I also needed to find a tenant whose rental payments would cover my costs on the new property. But taking this kind of summary action dispelled any fears related to the attendant financial risk because it suddenly created new possibilities for growth that I hadn't previously imagined.

My new house became a base from which I could change my work and the course of my life. I found it startling how making one bold decision presented such a promising template for future living. Once I had made the move, I scarcely gave my old life a second thought.

This transition also jibed with an important 21st century idea concerning livelihood. Increasingly, the structure of today's economy demands that more people do a variety of things, not go to an office or factory for eight hours a day and perform one task for one employer. Making a (satisfying) living in the future will involve not building a career, but creating multiple revenue streams, which simply means doing a few things we enjoy in order to sustain us. In sum, we must all run to daylight, not just to find our true selves but to create fresh opportunities in a fast-changing economy.

*Close the Deal.* In running a race or just out for a daily jog, get into the habit of going hard the last 100 yards. Finish strong; run through the tape, imagined or real. In tennis this is called "closing." A player develops the ability to "close out" a match – win when the contest is on the line – not just through his attitude in the heat of battle. He develops the closing habit by being serious when *nothing* is at stake – in practice.

## TRUE SPIRIT, TRUE SELF

I recall my first glimpse of Andre Agassi in the flesh on a practice court at a tournament in Los Angeles a few years ago. Even though Agassi was due to play later that evening, he was pounding every shot in what would amount to a short but serious warm-up. The word on Agassi is that an hour of practice with him is so intense that it feels like three hours with most other players. With Agassi there is no wasted time or motion. In practice he internalizes an intensity that will come naturally once the match is on, making it easier for him to close when the time comes.

The deeper meaning of Agassi's regimen is that he gets the most out of what he has. When you engage your inner resources in this concentrated manner, "control comes from within, it is not imposed from without," writes Haridas Chauduri. "The more we create interest in a healthy line of thinking or exploration of the outside world, the more we evoke a spirit of self-discipline."

Chauduri calls this quality "intelligent self-control," and it's important to develop it because, as he further notes, "much of our frustration and failure is due to a lack of knowing where we are going in life. However, once we have a positive sense of direction other things fall into place."

*Let the Fish Come to You.* If you make a habit of going to the ball and closing the deal then you will begin to create magic in your life. Good things will come your way. I noticed this phenomenon while snorkeling one afternoon with my younger son off Key West. After being in the water awhile, I realized that instead of my having to look for fish, they began to come my way. They seemed to be displaying a natural curiosity about me. It was as if they were acknowledging my presence in their world and the effort that I had made in coming to visit. Of course, if I had suddenly reached out to grab a fish they all would have immediately darted off.

In life, for things to come to us we must be sincere of mind and observant of our surroundings. And we must be calm and patient. There is a balance to be struck between going after something and putting in the hard work to get it, but not wanting it so much that we lunge at it. The moment we do so the object of our grasping eludes us.

If you make the right effort you will find that things will migrate your way, not all at once, but in a quietly sustained manner. This is the natural result of your work. What is important will eventually flow to you, and what is not will drift away.

**The Right Path Reveals Itself**

The man who gets into the arena and loves the battle sooner or later ends up playing his own deeper game because he knows he must. He must become his own man and find his own way. He competes against himself and his own benchmarks, spending little time comparing himself to others. In other words, he fights the right battles for the right reasons. This spares him the anguish of fighting the same wrong battles over and over again.

Creating and following your own path is never easy, but it is worth the struggle because it validates the self and enriches the community. By taking the requisite risks, the mavericks and seekers push us all forward. They open our eyes and give us courage. But the lone individual also carries a greater burden. He must find his own cues, steer his own course, and meet his own goals.

# TRUE SPIRIT, TRUE SELF

He must visualize his path and take it, often with little encouragement or help from others.

If, after careful thought, you cannot visualize what it is you think you want to do then it is not for you. The right path is the one that reveals itself after a requisite amount of considered reflection. It is something a person comes to imagine clearly, beckoning him on.

Some years ago I started an investment newsletter. I could visualize this publication fully, down to the layout, well before the first issue ever appeared. I knew what I wanted to say. I also believed in the organic worth of my idea and that an audience for this newsletter would, therefore, materialize. With no market research and an initial investment of less than $5,000, I launched the newsletter, which subsequently lasted for six years, with circulation eventually building to 5,000 subscribers.

Publishing that newsletter never made me rich, but it certainly worked as a business. Just as meaningful, I was able to forge a bond with my readers, some of whom corresponded with me regularly and even became personal friends. Among the most pleasing refrains I heard from them were words such as, "I like your philosophy," or "I like the way you think."

People who start businesses simply to make money suffer one of two fates. First, they don't make money. Second, they risk losing their sense of self. True success can only grow from within. It must take root in your being and sensibility. In other words, failure, financial or spiritual, reveals our inauthentic selves. It tells us who we are not meant to be and in the process nudges us in more hopeful directions. True success, no matter how small the monetary reward, affirms who we really are. It guides us along the right and fulfilling path.

**Stand Tall**

Authentic people take pride in themselves. "To belittle yourself is not modesty so much as stupidity," says Montaigne. "But to overpraise yourself is not only presumption, but folly."

Pride, religion teaches us, is a sin. I think that pride, in appropriate measure, is a virtue. It's as vital as air and water to a person's growth and success. If we do not like ourselves then how can we begin to live our lives in the full way we are intended to. We are not here to be egoless. Egolessness translates as the absence of form or structure. It is like having a body without a skeleton. We are here to craft strong, healthy, balanced, and supportive egos. We are here to stand tall and represent ourselves faithfully to others and to the universe.

"A human being needs self-respect, needs the experience of worthiness," writes Nathaniel Branden in *Honoring the Self: the Psychology of Confidence and Respect*. "We must act to achieve our goals – and in order to act, we must value ourselves as beneficiaries of our actions."

The mind that equates pride with sinfulness will often confuse a love of beauty with vanity. The two are very different, if not polar opposites. Beauty reaches out to touch and selflessly merge with the world. Vanity is endlessly self-regarding, closing in on the small, artificial world it fashions for its own comfort.

The trick is to ground pride in humility just as we would anchor beauty in modesty. Magnificent trees must bury their roots deep in the ground in order to reach so high. What is humility? It is the quiet knowledge of who you are; it is that groundedness which permits a person to soar. It is the sensibility that announces itself boldly – in the quietest of voices.

### Carry Yourself Well

Humility relates to cleanliness and propriety, not in an obsessive or puritanical way, but in something more organic. It is about dressing well – simply and neatly, but never extravagantly. It's about taking pride in your appearance.

A few years ago I wrote a magazine profile of Nick Saban, the head football coach at Louisiana State University. Saban had been hired to turn around the program at LSU. That happened quickly on the field, with the team going 8-4 in its first season under Saban, up from 3-8 the prior year. Three years later, LSU would win a share of the national championship. (Saban recently moved on to try his hand at reviving the Miami Dolphins, who recently came off a woeful 4-12 season.)

At LSU, Saban helped raise $10 million to build an academic center for athletes to increase their graduation rate. He brought in outsiders from FBI agents to psychologists to speak to the team about the pitfalls facing high-level college athletes. He cut down on the grueling pre-season practice schedule so as not to exhaust his players, while instituting a regimen of judo to improve balance and flexibility.

Saban, whose degree is in Psychology, told me that his aim was to round out his players' characters so they might take better actions, on and off the field. Referring to that objective, he said,

# THE SELF IN ACTION

"The choices you make, make you." When I asked Saban how he felt he was doing in changing his team's mindset he replied that the one change he was proudest of was the least measurable. "I'm told that our players carry themselves better," he said.

### 'Watch Yourself Hour by Hour'

Saban's words bring to mind one of Seneca's thoughts: "Be as respectful of yourself in private as you would be of others out in society. Watch yourself hour by hour because how you behave each day ordains how your life will unfold."

It's important to be conscious of your actions as you move through the day, especially as they affect others but even when you are alone. Make wise decisions even when no one is watching because, as Saban notes, the choices you make, in public or private, make you.

Lay out a schedule for yourself in the morning of the tasks to be done that day. Take time along the way to relax, but not waste time. Have a schedule but don't succumb to rigid patterns.

I stopped taking the newspaper in the morning because reading it over breakfast daily became too much of a habit, and it began eating into my vital morning hours. Instead, I decided that I would pick it up on the newsstand when I went out later in the day, three or four days a week, not seven. I also began reading the paper in the quiet of the late afternoon, the early evening, or even the following day. Deferring the pleasurable habit of reading the paper made it that much sweeter. More important, I wanted the newspaper to accommodate itself to my schedule, not the other way around.

## Be Precise

Aristotle offers similar advice in equating tempered behavior with virtue. This notion is contained in his "doctrine of the Mean," wherein he writes, "The equal part is a sort of mean between excess and deficiency." Aristotle's idea is that appropriate behavior is typically that balance point of moderation between the extremes that permits a person to act with a thoughtful precision.

When you eat by yourself cook a simple meal, sit down, and eat slowly as if you were in a nice restaurant. To be spirited and creative, cook with a knife, not a spatula, and let nothing go to waste. Run the larder down to near nothing and then create a meal from leftovers. You will be surprised how much you can do with so little.

Precision fits hand in glove with moderation. Aristotle tells us that establishing a sense of proportion in all areas of our lives encourages virtuous behavior. It trains us to think before we act and not to overreach. And yet, when we do reach we do so precisely, which is to say wisely and with purpose.

Acting proportionally fosters balance and consistency. Consistency – not "genius" or "talent" – produces favorable results. When we show up faithfully, when we build things patiently and with care, we one day find that we have gifted ourselves an estimable body of work. Any accomplished writer will tell you that three or four hours a day – every day – conscientiously applied to his craft will eventually yield a bookshelf full of titles bearing his name.

Conversely, if we don't stay at a task it inevitably drifts away from us. "The habit of digression – lack of continued interest –

want of fixed purpose, is an almost general failing," writes Robert Henri in *The Art Spirit*. "It is too easy to drift and the habit of letting oneself drift begets drifting. The power of concentration is rare and must be sought and cultivated." In other words, concentration on a task crystallizes it. Concentration (focus) is the energy that gives any undertaking not just its purpose and direction, but also the structure around which that endeavor can take form and grow.

You honor your work by staying with it. The same thing goes for your life. Do the vital tasks that need doing each day with commitment and willingness. See them as sacred. They, in turn, will sanctify your life.

### Grow From the Inside Out

Most people seek to impress others. It's more important to impress yourself. Look upon each day as an opportunity to be great based on your own standards, your own objectives. This is not egoism, narcissism, nor selfishness. It is self-recognition in action, the self at work.

Sooner or later, a person must come to terms with himself. He must like himself, must love himself really, no matter how much others may shun him or how little society may value his talents. Nathaniel Branden states this idea quite simply in *Honoring the Self: The Psychology of Confidence and Respect*. "Living up to my own standards is…an essential condition of self-esteem," he writes. "The notion that my self-esteem is simply a function of how others see and evaluate me is false."

Meet your obligations to yourself before you begin making

promises to others. Live through yourself and not through others. That means building yourself from the inside out. Grow your inner riches – character, intellect, soul – just as systematically as you would put savings in the bank.

In our modern culture we have grown obsessed with "looking good" and impressing others. We work feverishly on the outside and neglect the core. Consider the case of Jeffrey Skilling, the former CEO of Enron, with his Harvard MBA and well-buffed background as a management consultant. In his heyday, Skilling waxed poetic about the genius of Enron's complex business model. He would lecture the press on the model's uniqueness. When puzzled or skeptical reporters raised questions about how the business really worked, Skilling simply dismissed them, retorting that they "just didn't get it."

His demeanor brings to mind the likes of a Milosevic or a Castro, with their lengthy, lecturing – and hectoring – speeches, crowding out any prospect of dialogue. People who act in such didactic, not to mention bombastic, fashion are not to be trusted. People who cannot stand to listen live in fear of the truth, not to mention their own shadows. They make noise to drown out the resounding emptiness within.

When Enron fell apart and was exposed as the house of cards that it was all along, Skilling, the previously self-proclaimed overlord of the company's vaunted business model, claimed that he was unaware of any wrongdoing within Enron, and was, therefore, blameless. He sought all of the glory – and lucre – while shirking the responsibility. In the end, Skilling proved to be as hollow at the core as the company over which he presided.

# THE SELF IN ACTION

## Have the Courage to Think Honestly

The most trusted people, in contrast to the Skillings of the world, are those who claim no special expertise but are largely self taught through their well-developed awareness, humility, and sincerity. These are people who gain much of their learning through careful observation and diligent study. They are often as direct and as known to us as one signature name: Whitman, Emerson, Thoreau, Ghandi, Einstein, Lincoln, Roosevelt, and so on. They announce themselves through their wise work and evident humanity. They stand, first and foremost, accountable for who they are. In so doing, they discharge their responsibilities to others.

At some point in your life it's a good idea to muster the courage to tear up your resume and become known by your deeds, your art, your person. It is a tougher way to go because you must generate much of your own energy – while much of society will be clueless as to the significance of your message. But in the process you will come to know yourself fully. You will be solid at the core.

Think, for example, about Whitman and Thoreau, dismissed in their day as loafers and cranks. Yet they remained as unshakeable in their own self perceptions as in their visions of life. "I know I am august, I do not trouble my spirit to vindicate itself or be understood," wrote Whitman.

"Be wary of any enterprise that requires new clothes," Thoreau wryly warned about life in conventional society. Today, of course, *Walden* and *Leaves of Grass* are classics, essential reading for any student of American literature. And Thoreau and Whitman have much to tell us, including:

## TRUE SPIRIT, TRUE SELF

*The mission of any honorable, self-respecting person is to live an open life.* When you walk outside in the morning face the sun, raise your head, and square your shoulders to the day. Do that and the life force will enter you and light your soul. The open person has no fears – just as he has no airs.

*Project a bias toward measured action.* "Be bold in attack but never embark on an action without a clear end in view," wrote Marcus Aurelius. Taking bold action dispels fear. Assuming appropriate risk reduces risk.

*Do not undersell yourself.* We are here to be noble, majestic even. Being human is a great undertaking with great possibilities. I am talking about acting in a manner that is heroic, not vain. No preening or strutting, just carrying ourselves through each day, and thus through life itself, with a native dignity. As Robert Henri writes, "When people have the courage to think honestly, they will live honestly, and only through a transparent honesty of life will a new civilization be born."

### Honesty Begins with Silence

People can speak truthfully, and live honestly, as Henri suggests, only when they establish a ground of silence in their lives. You must first listen in order to hear. If you cannot hear how can you really hope to speak in a clear voice?

Brad Gilbert, former coach to the tennis stars, Andre Agassi and Andy Roddick, counsels in his book, *Winning Ugly*, that when playing a tennis match a player should elect to receive serve first.

His idea is that your opponent may not be fully warmed up. If you break his serve then you have quickly gained an edge. If you have not, then nothing is immediately lost.

While conversation, unlike a tennis match, is not a competition, it is a good idea to "receive" first. Let the other person speak; hear him out. By listening before speaking you have more information – the product of two minds – to work with.

Listening is selfless. It springs from silence and quietude; a consciously cultivated receptivity. When we have developed the ability to listen we can speak in a quiet, unhurried voice.

A quiet voice equates with a quiet mind. In tennis, knowledgeable people speak about good players having "quiet" or "soft" hands. Quiet hands are precise hands. And precise hands might be thought of as "philosophical" hands. "Philosophy is good advice and no one can give advice at the top of his voice," writes Seneca. We need to sow our words like seeds, judiciously, and tend the ideas that spring from them so they will display their inherent abundance.

**Responsibility is Freedom**

When you speak and write simply and directly, when you have a predisposition to listening, it informs your whole life. You ground your pride in a benign disposition. "Straightforwardness and simplicity are in keeping with goodness," says Seneca. A simple life steers us clear of deception and toward virtue.

Practicing simplicity puts you on the path to personal freedom. Freedom is not the absence of responsibility, but the presence of directed will. Evolved people do not seek freedom from responsibility, but freedom through responsibility. Choose your tasks carefully, and then take full charge of them. Don't do things you don't intend to complete. Don't take on projects that other people tell you are your "duty." That is prelude to bondage.

### Delight in Your Mastery

Some people sidestep responsibility and its liberating possibilities. They program themselves, instead, to pursue pleasure because that is what comes most easily to humans. People generally like to feel good, the more often the better. But doing what comes easy can create difficulty, just as the mindless pursuit of passing pleasure can play out as enduring pain.

Pleasure should not be the goal, but the byproduct of striving toward it. When we gain this understanding we stop searching for pleasure and, instead, find joy and contentment through our efforts.

Just as science now informs us that there are so-called "good" and "bad" fats, to find true pleasure requires courting the "good" sort of pain that comes with pushing yourself. Good pain accompanies thorough and honest exertion. Bad pain, conversely, arises from anxiety, anger, and fear. Avoidance, the unwillingness to assume responsibility and recognize reality, compounds bad pain.

What is the prescription for bad pain? Exercise body and mind daily so that feeling good pain becomes a habit. Soon enough we don't even experience such exertion as "painful." It is just how we live.

In yoga, the term for such regular effort is "practice." By sustaining our practices we "deepen" them. That blurs the imaginary

## THE SELF IN ACTION

line we draw in our minds between pleasure and pain by pushing our strength through our perception of pain.

By pushing against pain with awareness we draw possibility into the foreground of our lives. We come in touch with our mastery and delight in it. We welcome whatever "pain" we feel because we know it makes us stronger and wiser. Good pain, when accessed through regular, mindful practice, is the daily medicine of life.

CHAPTER FOUR

# RELATIONSHIPS

**Strive to Self-Actualize**

We forge identity through our relationship to our environment and to others. The psychologist, Abraham Maslow, refers to the well-formed identity as the "self-actualized" personality. The path to self-actualization leads through the mass of people, or what Maslow calls "the herd." Early in life we orient by the herd to gain safety, approval, and a sense of self. While the herd may protect us in the short term, in the long run it cannot fully sustain us. We need to move away and assume more responsibility for our own growth.

Risk increases the more we move out to the edges of the herd, but so, too, does possibility. It is only when we become sure enough of self and identity that we can begin to migrate away from the center, and as we move toward the periphery we begin to encounter the freedom that makes self-expression possible.

Maslow sees the herd as comprised of about 75% of the population, with most of the balance, roughly 20%, being what he calls "individuated." That leaves a small minority that, by Maslow's reckoning, ever self-actualizes. This group consciously displays what he refers to as "being values." Maslow identifies 15 being values, which include such qualities as: aliveness, wholeness, fairness, beauty, playfulness, honesty, and self-sufficiency.

This fraction of the population that puts being values into practice are the people who live their lives in creative, thoughtful, and original ways. It can include poets, philosophers, and artists. But it can just as easily include short order cooks, street sweepers, and morticians.

One of the most spirited people I ever met was my dentist in California, the appropriately named Dr. Lippi. He took a craftsman's pleasure in working on my teeth, delightedly comparing them to small gears. What matters here is not the "what" but the "how." The zest and commitment we bring to life ultimately defines us in the eyes of others.

The fully actualized man is the philosopher in our midst. He is not, despite popular myth, a learned sage or ponderous pedagogue. Quite the contrary. He is a genuine and pragmatic liver of life, intent on squeezing the most he can from it. He is:

*Curious:* He knows that life offers deep yet simple truths – and he seeks them out.

*Honest:* He is truthful. He knows that by practicing honesty (openness) he draws positive energy in to achieve uncommon feats.

*Judicious:* He listens first and responds in a quiet manner. He is open to other viewpoints. He respects facts and honors context.

RELATIONSHIPS

*Striving:* He understands that effort makes the difference between success and failure. By focusing on process, not outcome, he trusts that the well-made effort will yield the right result.

*Caring:* He cares about what he does and how he does it. He cares for other people and is aware of how his actions affect them. But he will not needlessly sacrifice himself for others.

*Competent:* He knows his limits and works on his strengths and weaknesses alike. He is good at what he does.

*Firm:* He is purposeful, yet understated. When asked, he expresses his opinion clearly, yet quietly. He calmly stands his ground while doing no harm.

The fully actualized man announces himself simply to others. His positions are well considered, and his character is an organic outgrowth of what he thinks and believes. While he relates readily to the herd, he declines to be influenced by convention because he is secure in his own well-crafted rules. He lives, above all, free of fear.

**Convert Power Into Strength**

The aware man, like it or not, can become a target for the envy, fear, and resentment of others. They wish they could be like him, a free man. He may even find himself preyed upon by those who would steal his energy simply to bring him down. In extreme cases, notably police states, he will be subject to imprisonment, torture, and even death. Don't let other people pull you down; if they seek to do so they might as well be trying to drown or bury you. Resist them for your own survival.

Safeguarding your energies in this vital way helps create your boundaries. Boundaries demarcate the autonomous, sovereign self. They outline the domain of the individual. Surround yourself with people who respect your boundaries. Move away from people who encroach on them. And remember this:

*Despairing people infect others with their own misery.* Many people need to offload and project their negative energy onto others. Give them half a chance, and they will do just that.

*Power is a poor substitute for talent.* When people fail to develop their own talents they often seek to dominate those who have. The wrongful exercise of power expropriates the energy of others. There is nothing creative or original about that. History tells us that the most power-hungry of men are willing to destroy millions of other people's lives in a desperate effort to fill their own empty one. Powerful people can be the least creative among us. As a result, they can be the least humane.

*Don't confuse power with strength.* People begin to transmute power into strength when they forsake the need to control others. But many people who exercise power have little idea how to convert it into strength, nor do they have much incentive. The strong man, conversely, has developed the capacities of sensitivity and empathy. The powerful man struggles to practice these virtues because he sees them as limiting, when, in fact, they promise liberation. The author and professor of religion, James Carse, makes an important distinction between these two concepts in his book, *Finite and Infinite Games*. To Carse, power is limiting, while strength is boundless. He writes:

> A powerful person is one who brings the past to an outcome, settling all its unresolved issues. A strong person is one who carries the past into the future, showing that none of its issues is capable of resolution. Power is concerned with what has already happened; strength with what has yet to happen. Power is finite in amount. Strength cannot be measured, because it is an opening and not a closing act.

## Subtract Creatively

Sincerity helps a person thrive as an individual. Sincerity is not about seriousness, nor solemnity. It is about caring – about yourself, about others, about whatever you take on. It is about consciously being in touch with all that touches you.

Insincerity is a form of falsity and capitulation. It creeps in when people lose the capacity to feel for others. One sees it in large organizations, where individuals can hide out, shirk responsibility, grasp for power, and ultimately ignore people's real needs. The United Nations is a case in point. There, lifetime bureaucrats, corrupted by Iraq's bogus Oil for Food program, turned a blind eye to the suffering of ordinary Iraqis.

The true individual, the committed soloist, lacks this kind of institutional "cover." More exposed to the rigors of competition, he cannot deflect accountability. He has little choice but to represent his own simple truth to the world, taking what he does seriously while still cultivating a lightness of spirit. That keeps him balanced. He understands that the only jobs worth doing are those worth doing well – and so he does fewer things better. Those things he considers unimportant, trivial, and petty fall away. He creatively subtracts.

**Practice Sincerity**

Sincerity gives us the power to discriminate. We come to see the small, everyday untruths – the insincerities – that others tell for what they are. I am talking, for example, about the people who promise to return our calls and really have no intention of doing so, or those who habitually miss deadlines they pledge to meet. We come to understand that we should first cut these people some slack in the hope that their behavior might improve. Nudge them toward fairer dealings. In the event that doesn't work out, we should then quietly move on, with compassion. It's a little like getting served a bad meal at a restaurant. Rather than complain about the woeful service or uninspired cuisine, simply tell yourself that there are other establishments that merit your patronage.

The larger point is that we should not sacrifice ourselves to others' lesser standards or to their manipulations, nor should we scorn or belittle people who we feel do not measure up. Rather, we simply say, "This relationship is not for me." We bid it adieu, always with thanks for whatever good it did produce.

Such a situation befell me a few years ago after I had signed

# RELATIONSHIPS

a contract with a magazine to write an agreed-upon number of stories over the course of the ensuing year. But soon into the arrangement I realized that the editor had no intention of honoring that commitment. He struck me as evasive, scattered, and feckless. (Entrenched in his important job in a big-city skyscraper, he also seemed well-buffered from my concerns.) I did my best to fulfill my end of the bargain, but to no avail. I finally ended up walking away from close to $20,000 worth of work that I had expected to come my way.

I was at first angry and frustrated over what I saw as a lack of professionalism on this man's part. While I didn't see his actions as necessarily willful, I felt that he should have assumed more responsibility for them. But the minute I walked away from the relationship I stopped feeling victimized. I consciously decided that I simply would not look back; I had more fruitful opportunities to tend to. And once I did that I felt immediately better and didn't give that editor and his magazine a second thought.

Alas, there are more situations in life than we realize from which we should calmly disengage. What holds us back is the perception that doing so will cost us, if not monetarily then emotionally. But each time we pay the price and let go of something that we instinctively know we should release we free ourselves to reach toward something worthier. New, better, and truer things come into our lives.

By this process the sincere man comes to keep the company of his own kind. He knows that he really has no other choice because with insincere – and patently false – relationships the cost escalates the longer they continue. When not addressed, such arrangements devolve into situations that become downright unaffordable.

### **Settle Up, Not Down**

People talk about "settling down" in their lives as if doing so is a long cherished goal, the end to the quest. It's important to grow up and be responsible, but it's equally urgent that we not get too settled in our ways. When we do that we are apt to get mired.

Some people who settle down are really giving up. They are proponents of the rush to get married, have children, and assume debt. Those who hurl themselves into the wrong kinds of "commitments" (which, in fact, are really obligations or attachments) develop a vested interest in seeing others similarly burdened.

What matters is heeding those voices less and trusting your own instincts more. Assume the right responsibilities in the right order. Educate yourself before you choose a career. Develop your career before you get married. Become best friends with your spouse before you have children. There is a natural order and unfolding to life, but you cannot discern it if your training and education is not similarly ordered. Without cultivating the intelligence that is uniquely yours, your life will lack a sound foundation and, therefore, be vulnerable to collapse when under duress.

Some years ago I lived next to a woman whose backyard was a wildly overgrown mess. This was something I gave little thought to – the state of her garden, after all, was her affair – except when she would comment on what a hard worker, my best friend and able gardener, Karen, was. Her real message, not exactly subtle, was this: "Slow down; you're making me look bad."

# RELATIONSHIPS

People like this are to be kept at a distance, and quietly ignored, as well-meaning and friendly as they might appear. Their basic agenda is to bring us down – ever so skillfully – to their level in order to affirm their – stunted – worldview. They set a lower standard because it gives them comfort. Conversely, people who project higher standards discomfit them. When you lower your standards to make others feel better you end up lowering yourself. You grant yourself permission to fail.

## Learn as You Teach

It's important to set high yet realistic standards for yourself. Part of that process involves associating with people of a similar bent. "Our will needs to be inspired to stay consistently strong, and that inspiration comes best from those who are genuinely committed to the same objective," writes Tim Gallwey, in *Tennis: Playing the Inner Game*. "Those who play the inner game of life benefit in the same way by sharing dedication and experience with those of similar commitment."

Gallwey's idea is a simple one. When two players of equal commitment enter a contest they become engaged in a higher form of competition, wherein each player draws out the other's potential. "Winning" in this context becomes a footnote to the quality of the competition.

Seneca echoes Gallwey's thought, writing, "Associate with people who are likely to improve you. Welcome those whom you are capable of improving. The process is a mutual one: learn as they teach."

A few years ago, I had a regular tennis game with a top-ranked

# TRUE SPIRIT, TRUE SELF

player in New England. For a full year we practiced hard, honing our strokes and court tactics. The discipline of our workouts committed me to improving my game.

Then we began playing sets. This man, whom I came to consider my friend, would beat me routinely, but slowly I improved enough to give him a game and even win an occasional set. When that happened, the magic between us evaporated. I could see how much he hated to lose, even now and then. In time, he stopped returning my calls to play tennis.

It was frustrating. He had helped me lift my game, but at the moment when I was in a position to perhaps help and grow his (and him) he just walked away. He had been a great practice partner, but his ego had become hooked on the routinely easy wins. The casualty was our association and friendship, not to mention the delight of our mutual practice.

## Keep Aiming Higher

Keeping the company of people who challenge and test us prepares us for uncommon success. As we hold ourselves and others to high – and progressively higher – standards, good things result. These include:

- *We get into the habit of aiming higher. Pushing ourselves becomes second nature.* The tasks we take on no longer feel like work as we push through them and test our limits.

- *We shed our fear of losing.* Mentally minimizing the prospect of losing is a big part of winning in sports or in life. True champions find a way to win, no matter the odds because they come to play the game fully and put complete trust in the quality of their effort. They are never out of the contest because their high level of commitment focuses their energies where they belong – on the process.

– *We gain competence.* Thinking not just positively but proactively becomes our bias. We take things on in an orderly fashion and get them done with dispatch. When we get into the habit of doing things efficiently we also get better at looking out and seeing what is coming our way. We become better prepared for any and all eventualities.

## Make Friendship 'Fine and Noble'

Choose your friends wisely. You need fewer than you think.

Many of us surround ourselves with too many "friends" in order to feel "happy" and assuage the prospect of loneliness. It's important to discriminate in our choice of friends because as we move upward in life we place an increasingly higher premium on the quality of our relationships. We need fewer but better ones.

Avoiding bad relationships saves vital psychic energy because it spares us the effort required to manage and eventually extract ourselves from them. Developing healthy relationships avails us of the positive energy that inevitably flows from such associations.

Montaigne, the great French thinker and essayist, placed friendship at the pinnacle of human relations, writing, "Of a perfect society friendship is the peak." Elaborating on that idea, he further wrote, "All those relationships that are created and fostered by pleasure and profit, by public or private interest, are so much the less fine and noble, and so much the less friendships, in so far as they mix some cause, or aim, or advantage with friendship."

True friendship is disinterested. It neither offers nor receives anything other than the friendship itself. (There is no such thing as a "business friendship." Similarly, we call those closest to us "personal friends" for good reason.) True friends are willing to share everything and ask for nothing in return. So when making friends it's a good idea to invest ample time on the front end. Do your due diligence to ensure that would-be friends are not approaching you with undue needs or unspoken agendas. Examine your motives in a similar light. Then commit fully. As Seneca writes: "After friendship is formed you must trust, but before that you must judge."

### Grow With Your Friends

Life is about growth and change. Some people change readily, while others resist it, and in the process slow down those around them. True friends will stay with you because they understand the nature and pace of change in you and adjust accordingly. They are in synch with your rhythms and attuned to your feelings. I mean this quite literally. My best friend, the woman with whom I live, will often be thinking the same thing at the same time as I am. Through our desire to share so much we have even come, it seems, to combine some of our mental wiring.

Don't be afraid to let go of the "familiar" person if the rela-

# RELATIONSHIPS

tionship feels too comfortable and fails to spur you on to greater things. Encouraging complacency in others is hardly the mark of true friendship.

Looking back on my life, I have no remaining true friends from childhood, and very few from my school years. My best friends now have been made through more recent associations and circumstances. This makes sense to me. To begin with, I am not much of a sentimentalist as I feel that getting too attached to our memories can get in the way of us taking positive present actions. I am also a different person now than I was 10 and 20 years ago. I should expect to have different friends – or old friends who have renewed themselves by growing alongside me.

Often old friends can become very different people from one another simply because they grow apart as time progresses. This is a natural process. People's needs and interests change; we should feel as free to go as we did when we came. It is just as natural, and just as common, as two people growing together.

So don't mourn the loss of an old friend. It may well be a sign of your personal growth. And remember, your truly best friends will be your best friends for life.

### Make Respect Mutual

We often underestimate the challenge of moving beyond the people who will slow us down, or even bring us down. Discriminate in choosing allies. It's time well spent.

The surest way to do that is to insist on fairness and reciprocity in your relationships. If others have no intention of treating you fairly, then move on. People whom I must call nine times out of ten get pushed down my list of "friends" into "acquaintance" territory because the energy required to sustain the relationship is out of balance. When insincerity and small untruths enter the mix we should lessen our reliance on the relationship.

Similarly, if you have no interest in working with someone beyond mere expediency – using their energy to your ends – then you owe it to both them and yourself not to continue the relationship. You are taking undue advantage. In this context, "respect" is meaningless unless it is mutual. Unfairly appropriating another person's energy is a form of stealing. Stealing another person's energy eventually returns to rob you.

**Turn Family Into Friends**
In today's political climate "family values" are often seen as an unquestioned good. Yet despite our best efforts to idealize them, families can often be not much more than a disparate group of individuals who happen to be joined by blood. Those things that divide families – rivalry, jealousy, and pettiness – can often corrode the ties that bind them.

At its root, family is clan, and clan is tribe. The tribalism we see wreaking havoc in the world today impedes the building of larger civil societies founded on trust, merit, and objectivity. Most "families" – the Cosa Nostra, for example – seek undue advantage for their members, while demanding blind loyalty from them. Families can often be more about favoritism than fairness. They can be undemocratic.

For families to truly flourish they should be informed by a strong sense of fairness and reciprocity. Maybe if we spent more energy liking our brothers, as opposed to loving them, it would help. Perhaps it would be healthier if families resembled a society of friends, where harmony through respect is held up as the highest value. This could define the strong family and make it the true building block of healthy community.

### Commit; Don't Attach

True friends share completely. Basing their relationship on the full and free exchange of all things, they bring a sense of flow and ease to the arrangement.

My best friend and I both feel that our friendship, by its genuineness and sincerity, transcends marriage. Marriage can be daunting, as it often carries the weight of considerable expectations. Consider some of the language used to describe it; words such as "institution," "bond," "covenant," and "contract," to name a few. The two of us already share everything we have, most notably our souls. I do not use the word "equitably" here because it implies a division of property, responsibilities, and the like; all of which are up for debate and negotiation. Marriage should be about consensus and unity.

In our modern, materialistic society many of our dealings, even those intended to be intimate in nature, are based either on an implicit quid pro quo, or worse, forced exchange. "No one can lead a happy life if he thinks only of himself and turns everything to his own purposes," says Seneca. "You should live for the other person if you wish to live for yourself. A person who shares much with a fellow human being will share everything with a friend."

True friendship promotes sharing, and in so doing teaches

us a central idea of Stoic philosophy: A meaningful life is founded on the notion of forsaking attachment for commitment. The Stoics tell us that friendship does not necessarily hold out some sort of "good," or reward, in the form of, say, an end to loneliness or unhappiness. The potential benefit is more tied up in what we learn about ourselves in the process of making friends and serving them. We learn that we must love in order to be loved. We should, similarly, make friends not to be happy, but to have the opportunity to share the happiness that we, ourselves, have created.

This idea contains no small measure of faith. If we entrust our happiness to another, with no expectation of getting a like measure back, then we, in fact, stand a better chance of being returned that person's happiness. Conversely, if friendship devolves into a "deal" then we run the risk of either feeling shortchanged or driving the other person away because he or she feels cheated. Contracts carry the weight of often unrealistic – and enforced – expectations. They invite imbalance. True friendships, which transcend contracts, carry no such burdens because they are voluntary and free of conditions. They become a healthy means of acting toward, and living with, another person.

### True Friendship is Confident

Remember, marriage is not about entering into a contract, or even forging a bond. It is meant to be something quieter, softer, and more generous than that. But often marriage implies a pooling of resources, a merging of assets as a bulwark against a competitive world. That can harden a marriage.

Often to ensure survival and assuage loneliness we rush into marriage. It becomes almost a default way of living. People get married because they can, and because society approves. That makes marriage less of a social ideal than a social convention. Some of us, no doubt, like the arranged and sanctioned nature of marriage because we prefer order to happiness.

We should aim to break that cycle by replacing marriage's formalistic nature with the simplicity of friendship. A true friendship frees its participants to actualize their individual selves, the sum of which can be invested in the relationship for their common benefit. Friendship is a confident, not an embattled or codependent, relationship. It stresses the merging of positive energies in order to expand and more fully share experience, not to defend against possible adversity. Friendship is open in nature, whereas marriage can close in on itself, limiting its possibilities in the process.

### Guide, Don't Judge

Another arena in which we can practice commitment without attachment and realize great benefits is in the rearing of children. Attachment is another form of seeking control. In our urge to control our own, often chaotic, lives we end up seeking to control our children because we hold power over them. We turn independent and teachable human beings into objects and possessions.

For the most part, good parents do not tell their children what to do. They show them how to live by living well, themselves, and speaking truthfully. Living well is like writing well. It is clear and direct, yet also implicit. It conveys meaning. The ideas emerge through the strength, clarity, and grace of the prose. Good writing does not tell; it shows.

That's what raising children is all about. Show your children that you are a loving, compassionate, dignified, and principled human being, and they will come to you. They can usually figure out the rest because children, generally more flexible of mind than adults, are more observant than we give them credit for. You will earn their curiosity, and their unvoiced respect. Like always attracts like.

Speaking softly and acting wisely also teaches your children to be intuitive. Instructing, preaching, and ordering convey rigidity. That instills fear and discourages risk-taking. Rigidity pushes children away as it constricts the flow of energy between parent and child. Children want to be listened to and acknowledged. They want to be guided, not judged.

At the same time, it is important to speak clearly with your children. That is the parent's prerogative – and true responsibility. Quiet honesty and a certain firmness of character will, in time, get your children's attention. The rebellious teenage years will pass. At that point, most children, eager to be seen as adult peers, circle back to their parents. (I lived at home one year when I was in my early 20's and recall with pleasure the intellectual companionship of my parents.) How readily they return depends a lot on how deftly their parents handled them in prior years.

Raising children, like living itself, is an endlessly delicate balance between letting things come to you and of going after them. Many people struggle to find that balance. They are either too grasping, or too passive and entitled. Their greed eats them up, or their indolence allows life to roll over them. Search out that crucial balance as a parent. Learn from your children as you teach them, and you will gain friends for life.

### Sex is Art and Art is Sex

Sex is about two people being, and becoming, complete equals. What is given is received in equal measure. As with children, a keen sense of reciprocity informs the healthy sexual relationship.

If sex was meant to be only for procreation nature wouldn't have given us such a surplus of reproductive raw material. Sex is just as much about finding the deepest pleasure possible, joy. Sex is, therefore, a worthy pastime – in addition to being the most humanly creative act possible. It's a good way to spend some time with someone you love.

We are now discovering that a good sex life is an integral component to good physical and mental health. We are learning about "sexual intelligence" and how some people are more adept than others at tapping into their sexual energy and turning it to fruitful use.

Good sex comes through true – intelligent – friendship. It relies on openness. Sex should be partaken of not furtively and in the dark, but joyfully and in the open, where the nakedness of each partner symbolizes the honesty they bring to the relationship.

Men and women who know how to effect this unity are more apt to find happiness because this spirit of openness informs the moments between them. This is the essence of love, the absence of secrets multiplying the prospects of mystery between lovers.

## TRUE SPIRIT, TRUE SELF

If two people are in love they should be prepared to grab each other at any (feasible) moment and act on their impulses. A strong sense of physicality – in private moments – enlivens any friendship. (Conversely, public displays of affection are often inappropriate and off putting to others.) If more people took this spirit of spontaneity to heart and joined their energies whenever possible it would dissolve a lot of marital discord, not to mention geopolitical tension.

But sex is easily displaced by lesser substitutes because it demands honesty, and, therefore, real spiritual effort. (It is curiously ironic that sex, so immediately physically gratifying and therefore seemingly effortless, is, in fact, anything but easy due to its inevitably weighty emotional component.) What are those proxies? I'm talking about losing oneself to excess in work, food, entertainments, or chemical palliatives. We draw these diversions to us in order to displace the hard emotional work any sound relationship requires.

Sex, like everything else in life, is simply its own unique form of energy. When shared wisely between two loving people, that energy multiplies throughout their common lives, building an easy abundance that will never diminish.

### Close the Circle of Creative Joy

By the conventional way of thinking we are ashamed of our flesh, our essential selves. So we often fail to take good care of it. We disconnect work first from the body, and then from the mind. It is worth noting that the Industrial Age overworked the human body to the point of exhaustion in dirty and dangerous physical

# RELATIONSHIPS

jobs. The Information Age consigns many of its workers to cubicles in sterile office buildings, where their bodies atrophy and grow heavy from lack of use. We can only hope for a future that transcends these two negative models of work. It's worth striving for, as I suspect that a healthier workforce might also result in a cleaner environment.

The path to that future begins with the individual living a full, physical life. Excercise daily and have sex with someone you love often. These two goals complement one another. They continually celebrate the body in its legitimate quest to reclaim its native right to sustained good health. Remember:

*People who have joyful and meaningful sex often stay younger longer* because in their honest intimacy they approach the life force.

*People who enjoy good sex usually find greater happiness than other people,* not just because they find more physical gratification, but because they encounter less guilt. Their honest passion burns it away.

*Sex is a wonderful form of recreation.* People with an evolved approach to sex see it as a form of recreation, a fruitful way to pass the time with someone they love. But they also see it as a means to re-creation, a healthful way of remaking the self and finding renewal.

*People who love each other have sex often because they love each other.* They close the circle of creative joy.

CHAPTER FIVE

# MAKING A LIVING

**Own Your Life**

It's a good idea to do as much as possible for yourself, rather than simply hire or rely on others. Invest your time, money, and energy in yourself and the vital aspects of your life. Doing things builds competence.

Competence creates the confidence that helps a person make his life his own. Self-assured people tend to be those who end up doing what they want to do in life. They are the ones who, as often as not, build their own businesses, create their own schedules, and pursue their own dreams.

Being the architect of your life can feel like a lonely pastime, but there comes a time in a person's life when he should well consider standing alone and investing as much as possible in himself. This is how we keep growing. Society is full of people who, Robert Henri says, are "living dying." Their existences, in effect, belong to other people, and whoever those "owners" are they will generally place a lower value on your life than on their profit and comfort. So investing in yourself in the broadest sense of the word

– consciously putting time, money, energy, and spirit into who you are and what you do – will set you on a wise course.

Strive, then, to give some time each day to what matters most to you. In completing this book, I committed myself to at least two hours of writing each day until the job was done, even though other, money-making pursuits called. This took place not over years, but over an intensive three-month period. It was through such focus that I was able to complete what to me was an important task, and in the process move my life to its next stage.

## Compete Against Yourself

Sustained commitment to tasks we love gives us an understanding that what matters is doing things well and fully. What doesn't matter is what others might think. When we work for ourselves or set our own course others may well comment or judge. Many people find ambition unsettling. They'd just as soon see us fail in order to reinforce the status quo to which they cling. Compete against yourself and your own standards, as measuring yourself against others' benchmarks could throw you off course.

From an early age I played tennis to the exclusion of most other sports. I enjoyed its solitary and self-contained nature. I, and no one else, was responsible for how things turned out on the court. In the midst of the game, the tennis player has no coach or teammates to rely on. He may well be alone, but at least he takes charge of his fate.

Later in life, I took up writing for similar reasons. In addition to having facets that I found aesthetically pleasing, both pursuits strike me as boundless. No matter how much I excel, I can never approach "perfection." Tennis and writing, I know, will promise to fully engage and challenge me as long as I practice them, which I hope will be for the rest of my life.

### Create Your Own Line of Inquiry

It is also worth getting used to the idea of working for yourself and guiding your destiny for another, practical reason. Within the modern economy, it seems, fewer people are employable in the same jobs for shorter periods of time. You have to keep expanding your skills and pushing deeper into the next realm of competency. Create your own line of inquiry, and it will evolve into your own line of work.

### Be a Niche Person

In my travels as a journalist I have often been drawn in the off hours to what I call niche spaces: small shops, art galleries, out-of-the-way restaurants, and small hotels. Such venues offer spatial, and spiritual, refuge from our over-scaled, homogenized world. They are familiar places to which we can retreat.

In a similar vein, we should seek to become niche people, to work on those parts of ourselves that will establish a specialness that will attract others. In this quest it is useful to imagine oneself as a small enterprise. The mission then is to discover the "business plan" you carry within, decode it, and put it into practice. Such a plan tells us how we, figuratively speaking, will generate "sales," market ourselves, and produce a return on our self-equity. This is our natural edge in life.

If we ignore our unique talents and fail to cultivate them

then we forfeit selfhood and run our lives at a "loss" that compounds with time. Developing what is unique about us provides the necessary energy to craft lives we can fully own. Resolve to be different and special. Don't try to please everyone. Do that and you will create the appropriate "markets" for your skills.

## Be a Steward of Your Own Affairs

While niches are hard to crawl into, they offer shelter and sustain unique life forms. If you set out to become a niche person then you stand a better chance of becoming secure in your calling and allowing your identity a chance to form. If you stand out on the plain of conformity then at first you may feel safe and protected by the herd, but eventually you will be exposed to the rigors of the environment.

The herd may offer temporary cover – and the illusion of safety – but its members are always jostling, worrying, and trampling one another. Anyone who has ridden the subway in New York at rush hour would understand this. There is nothing like a crowd to make a person feel alone and vulnerable. Conversely, two strangers meeting on a wilderness trail usually seem to share an immediately cordial, if not friendly, bond.

In its collective search for self-preservation, the herd perpetually culls itself. People join large groups and go to work for large organizations, mistaking their scale for security. Many of those who accept that bargain exchange autonomy and identity for the presumption of safety. But once the deal has been sealed, many organizations, which feel their strongest allegiance to their own perpetuation, grow emboldened. They begin to encroach on your security – your health insurance, your job, and even your pension. In such relationships, loyalty is hardly the constant, as advertised. It is one of the first casualties.

I experienced this dynamic a few years ago after leaving a small magazine where I had happily worked for 13 years, and where I had been well-recognized and rewarded for my efforts. I decided it was time to leave because the magazine had been sold to a multinational media concern for a large sum, $200 million, near the peak of the Internet boom. I knew I would be unable to have much allegiance to my new, distant, and faceless employer. I also knew a strong sense of loyalty could not be returned by a company needing to generate a respectable return on its large investment in the midst of a tough economy. It was time to move on and find a new niche.

I went from there to work under contract for two magazines owned by the world's largest media company, AOL-Time Warner, which, itself, had just been through a costly and equally flawed transaction. That was a mistake. AOL and Time Warner had merged, putting stress on the newly joined enterprise and costing shareholders billions in lost stock market value. The "contracts" I had signed were soon given shortshrift. The company was slow to pay me for work I had completed. More frustrating, no one in the organization seemed to really care about my contracts and whether their terms were actually being fulfilled. The editors with whom I worked either seemed to be running scared, trying to impress their bosses, or jostling for position in the hierarchy. They had focused much of their psychic energy inward on the key task of self-preservation in an organization under stress.

As dismaying as this situation was, it proved to be a worthy lesson, as it acquainted me with the reality of what can happen when individuals attempt to engage with large enterprises. (They end up having to observe the house's rules, which, of course, are skewed in the house's favor.) Equally important, it spurred me on to the next vital chapter of my life in which I resolved to become the steward of my own affairs. That would take precedence over all other "contracts," no matter how solemn or secure they may have seemed.

### A Sense of Value Creates Value

Stewardship is a healthy mindset because it eases our grasp on things. It invites us to become less possessive, making us more relaxed in the process.

The essential message of stewardship is that nothing really belongs to us. We are here for a short time, and whatever we nominally own will soon enough pass to someone else. So it is a good idea to not get too attached to our things. Rather, we should tend them with a mind to passing them on, even if they might eventually pass into the hands of strangers.

If we really own nothing then we cannot truthfully call ourselves "owners." Life intends for us to be caretakers, literally, of things that come our way. A good steward does not collect more things than he can care for and appreciate. By being a judicious and discriminating owner the steward understands value. When we value our things we similarly realize good value from them in an economic sense. We get a lot out of what we have. Our possessions reward our stewardship with pleasure and utility.

### Appreciate Craft

Owning and valuing a few good things pushes a sense of appreciation into the nooks and crannies of your life.

I recently came across an old can of waterproofing shoe wax in my closet, left over from a hiking trip to Wales more than 20 years ago. When I opened the can, the wax inside was still in good shape, and I set to working it into the stitching of a pair of hiking boots that I had owned for at least a decade. This simple task made me happy, as it set me to appreciating both the reliability of my boots and the durability of the wax. The prospect of using the two in concert compounded my pleasure.

It's important to own a few good things, but it's more important to appreciate them by getting full and proper use from them. If you understand what you have and why you have it then your possessions will serve you well. You take care of them; they take care of you. You will never lack.

Similarly, when you can properly acknowledge the craftsmanship of others by getting in touch with the things you own, then it better disposes you to appreciate what others do for a living. Everyone should make something with his own hands. Strive to have regular physical, tactile contact with things even if it's simply washing your car or stacking firewood. It is these simple, yet immediate, encounters with the real that keep us real.

### Respect Your Money

"Grasping at self," according to Buddhist belief, is a root cause of human suffering. The term refers to any undue or disproportionate desire that knocks us off balance. When we engage in grasping behavior, the world grasps back. What you project to the world eventually gets returned to you. The generous person receives generosity, the greedy person receives shame (an impoverished reputation), and the foolishly open-handed person will be dogged by a wanton attitude toward money.

The 1990's spectacle of American executives pulling down outsized paychecks is a case in point. By overreaching, some of these people lost what was of greatest value to them, their good names. Long considered an icon of American business, Jack Welch, the former chairman of General Electric, tarnished his legacy by charging numerous perks to the company despite having a net worth in the hundreds of millions of dollars. Similarly, Martha Stewart used to charge such incidentals as cups of coffee to her company expense account, even though she had a net worth approaching $1 billion. (It will be interesting to now see if the experience of prison will temper such proclivities in Stewart.)

Some years ago, I met a man named Sada Cumber who had come to this country from Pakistan with little more than a camera. One of nine children and the son of a portrait photographer in a small village, Cumber landed a job as a photographer at a resort hotel in Florida, snapping portraits of tourists. In time, he came to own a chain of one-hour photo development shops in Texas. He prospered, he believed, because he saw himself running a "soul-based" business, where people came before profits. Cumber shared important financial information with his employees to improve operating performance. In one case, he simply gave partial ownership of one of his stores to its manager to reward this diligent employee for his superior efforts.

Cumber summed up his thinking about money by saying, "If you do not respect your money, it will not respect you." Money is a conscious energy, highly attuned to its owner's values and intentions. Accordingly, we must handle our money wisely for it to benefit us. Conversely, when mismanaged, our money's energy can easily turn against us and hurt us in many ways beyond merely depleting our pocketbook. We will, for example, feel shame and reduced self-esteem if we allow money to simply slip through our fingers.

### Let Things Run Their Natural Course

Just as we should spend money wisely, not squander it, we should invest our money, not hoard it. I use the term "investment" in the broadest possible sense to include not just traditional investments, but also payments to skilled professionals or tradesmen, or even the purchase of everyday items. In truth, most every expense, if made mindfully, is really an investment, as it carries with it the potential for appreciation.

The wise person doesn't make his money work for him. He allows it to work for him. In other words, he works with the energy money provides him. He does so by seeking a reasonable return on his money. He does not exhaust his money by demanding that it produce an undue return.

People who expect an undue return on their capital end up putting it at undue risk. Gambling, of course, is an extreme example of this, but so, too, was the stock market saga of the late 1990's. In those years, "investors" bid up share prices to lofty levels. When the bubble burst, it wiped out some $7 trillion in paper wealth. That loss, which in relative terms rivaled the market losses during the Great Depression, had its origins in the psychology of the 1990's. During that decade, people became habituated to annual portfolio returns of 30% and 35%, when the average per annum return on U.S. stocks over the past 200 years has been roughly 8%. By demanding too much from their money, many people, quite simply, wore it out. Greed, in other words, doesn't grow capital. It does the reverse; it destroys it.

That seems counterintuitive, as the presumed impulse behind greed is to maximize wealth. But when our motives are unsound the opposite of what we intend is often the result we reap.

By "unsound," I am talking about anything that is inauthentic; in other words, shallow, deceptive, shortsighted, or borne of naked self-interest. We have to patiently allow the energies available to us to work their will, not work miracles. That means letting things run their natural course. We do that by being mindful (aware) of that energy's potential, not wishful (delusional) about its powers.

This, by the way, is the reason why diets rarely work, while regular exercise and sensible eating lead to long term weight control. Diets are unnatural in that they are meant to trick the body. But the body is too smart for that. It can readily distinguish between artifice, or shortcut, and consistent, authentic action, which is nature running its true course.

### Live Lean

It's a good idea, no matter your circumstances, to live lean. This should be your daily bias. As the Stoic philosopher, Seneca, writes,

## MAKING A LIVING

"It's in time of security that the spirit should be preparing itself to deal with difficult times." When you are well off, think thrift. Seneca relates how in ancient Rome the wealthy typically had houses which contained dirt-floored quarters called "poor men's rooms," in which they might live one day of ten.

If you live "poor" in many small ways then you will be commensurately enriched as you go about your life. I try to consciously work thrift into the fabric of my days. I avoid wearing clothes that require dry cleaning. My uniform is typically jeans and a tee shirt, with extra layers added for cooler weather. When appropriate, I re-use paper towels, and I climb stairs two at a time, assuming that the practice will incrementally prolong my life. I never bypass pennies spotted on the sidewalk. In fact, I am on the lookout for them, believing that the found penny will bring a day of good luck, while the bypassed penny could signal a reversal in fortune.

When small daily gestures like these become habits they serve as focal points around which one can build not just a way of living, but a whole life. After all, we live good and true lives in mindful increments.

While it is vital to put down roots, it's just as essential that we not get too comfortable and satisfied with what we have and what surrounds us. It could all be gone tomorrow. So within our home place, that place where we feel safe and secure – whether it's inside our heads or our houses – it's important that we live lean, that we be prepared to spend some time, happily, in our respective poor rooms. Reduce clutter. We want to impress others with ourselves, not our possessions, and if our things overwhelm us then they will obscure us in the eyes of people we wish to befriend. In fact, those people will mistake us for our possessions, making it all the harder to forge sound relationships.

### Share the Bounty

It is our natural right to draw comfort from life. We are not here to suffer. Contentment is a virtue.

But neither are we here to mindlessly indulge ourselves. We should strive to live as open-heartedly as we can.

The travails of the world relate in good measure to our inability to spread the bounty around; to keep the money energy flowing. What obtains, instead, is a baby's grasping reflex. From an evolutionary standpoint, the human race, alas, is still in its infancy. Our prevailing instinct is to hoard things in a desperate effort to avert pain and forestall death. But this sort of reflex action only blocks the fruitful flow of energy from one person to the next and consequently raises tension between them. When conflict results, as it often does, creativity disappears, and all parties find themselves fighting over a rapidly diminishing amount of booty. (I am reminded of an old joke. Question: Why are academic politics so vicious? Answer: Because the stakes are so small.)

Devastation and impoverishment spread like a stain. There is nothing so empty of everything as the middle of a war zone. As it drives out the creative impulse, conflict also hastens the advance of death. I think that science will one day reveal to us that the hoarding instinct prematurely ages us biologically, as it is simply another form of stressful behavior. If humans could figure out how to effectively share we'd likely add another ten years to average life expectancies.

Any luxury should be looked upon as precisely that – something you could survive without. So if a luxury comes into your possession consume it readily and happily with friends, because having it around will whet everyone's appetite and satisfy no one's. When I think of Christmas what I find most pleasurable is not the exchange of gifts between individuals but the sharing of good food and drink among family and friends. The man with the cellar full of expensive wines kept under lock and key is really grasping after some lack in his life. But when he draws readily and graciously from that trove when guests arrive he understands that sharing broadens well-being.

We should seek comfort as proper antidote to our labors. But when we pursue luxury for ourselves we simply reveal our anxiety to the world. When a person's life becomes a succession of displays designed to impress others then it is a good bet that that life has failed to impress itself. Fancy clothes, flashy jewelry, and sleek cars amount to little more than disguises, intended to distract others from knowing who we really are.

### Greed Depletes the Soul

Money, like all forms of energy, is meant to flow through us. We take in what we need and pass along what we don't. Our aim is not to mindlessly give money away because charity without purpose is more a salve for the giver's conscience than the recipient's condition. Rather, the wise use of money combines giving, spending, and saving to produce the widest possible benefit.

Keeping the money flow going ensures an appropriate lightness to life. Conversely, if we gather too much money about us it depresses our souls. F. Scott Fitzgerald may have believed that you could never be too rich, yet he was wise enough to create "glamorous" characters whose stories were inevitably tragic.

Various illusions can befall the well-off when they cling overly to their money. "People are out to steal from me." "The wolf is at the door, even though I have millions in the bank." "The next deal must be bigger than the last for all of this to mean anything." In sum, "enough" never seems to be quite enough.

Until recently, Richard Strong was the head of a large mutual fund that bore his name. He boasted a personal net worth of $800 million, yet he succumbed to making a number of improper trades that netted him $1.6 million at his customers' expense. For his transgressions, Strong ended up paying a $140 million fine.

Wealthy people can find it hard to live a simple life because money has adulterated their definition of simplicity. They unwittingly develop excessive needs, which often translates as excessive neediness. The "richest" people in life, on the other hand, are not those with the most money, but those who make the wisest use of whatever resources, financial and otherwise, come their way. They have learned how to draw the most from life because they remain mindful of putting the most into it. They know intuitively that greed, and the wastefulness that often accompanies it, undermines happiness and depletes the soul.

### Consume Things

"You ask what is the proper limit to a person's wealth," writes Seneca. "First having what is essential, and second, having what is enough."

MAKING A LIVING

As we wisely use energy in all endeavors we develop a sound view of limits; of what is "essential" and what is "enough." It is important to consume things as completely and as efficiently as possible, whether it's your physical energy applied to a given task, or your money directed at your financial responsibilities.

I play a small game with the contents of my refrigerator, intending to use up whatever it contains with a goal of zero spoilage. I find a neat and near empty icebox more calming than one groaning with food, some of which I know will inevitably go to waste. Such a mindset offers me the opportunity to go to the market often. I'll take $40 and buy groceries for the next few days. Shopping, just like ordering what I have in the icebox, thus becomes a similarly playful and creative endeavor as it creates a sense of abundance within bounds.

If one is a "consumer," and all of us in western society are, then we should consume in the literal sense of the term. We should use – and use up so they disappear – those perishable things around us. We should be like a raging forest fire, consuming everything in its path to usher in vibrant new growth. Doing so does not invite scarcity. Quite the contrary, it promotes sufficiency, which is abundance proportionate to need.

### Take What You Need

It is perhaps no coincidence that "miser" is the root of "miserable," or that Scrooge, the most miserly of men, is one of fiction's most recognized characters and enduring archetypes.

If we collect too much money around us it burdens the mind and afflicts the soul. Money, being really about flow, must keep moving, and it also must be routed to the right places, just like blood flow to the body. Hoarding is a malady that dogs the world. Many governments, sadly, amount to organized crime syndicates that steal from the populations they purport to represent and protect. In America, hoarding typically takes more "democratic" forms – in excessive executive pay packages, or, say, in the obesity epidemic, which largely afflicts the poor. Deprived and anxious in a sea of plenty, many less-advantaged people seek comfort in what they can readily obtain – cheap, mass-produced, high calorie food. Meanwhile, stick-thin, upper middle class women drive three-ton sport utility vehicles over well-paved roads to suburban supermarkets because they, too, feel embattled by the world around them.

When a few people hoard it often creates hardship, if not outright suffering, for many. Look at the rapacious rule of Saddam Hussein. Just ask the rank and file employees of Enron, who had their pension plans filled disproportionately with company stock – at the repeated urgings of, and with the repeated assurances from, the company's most senior managers. Enron is now bankrupt, and its equity is worthless due to the malfeasance of those very same managers. Taking more than we need for ourselves is more than hoarding. It is stealing.

We should all remember that Scrooge's story ends with transformation and thus hope. The man who thought he had everything suddenly realized he had nothing. And by giving up something, he was returned much.

CHAPTER SIX

# CRAFTING A LIFE

### Keep Company with Life

We Americans tend to see happiness as a birthright, yet for many of us genuine happiness remains elusive, as we often confuse it with pleasure. In the process, we divide the working self from the self at rest, assuming that the two function at cross purposes. We work to find release from our labors. We release to gird ourselves for the next round of work.

*Flow: The Psychology of Optimal Experience,* by Mihaly Csikszentmihalyi, is, in part, an exploration of the nature of happiness. Csikszentmihalyi's basic idea is that we find a deeper happiness when we experience a phenomenon he calls "flow." Flow, writes Csikzentmihalyi, is "the state in which people are so involved in an activity that nothing else seems to matter." He cites the example of a 76-year-old woman in the Italian Alps, where "the most striking feature of such places is that those who live there can seldom distinguish work from free time." As this woman goes about her day she describes a seamless regimen that breeds a strong affinity with her surroundings. "Serafina knows every tree, every boulder, every feature of the mountains as if they were old friends," writes Csikszentmihalyi, who then quotes her as saying, "I talk to everybody – plants, birds, flowers, and animals. Everything in nature keeps you company."

One of the more engaged people in his work that I know is a former neighbor of mine, Coleman Hoyt. Hoyt is a car dealer, and an honest, funny, and able one at that. He enjoys his work, and it shows in his broad knowledge of the car business. One piece of career advice that Hoyt recently gave my older son was to "get close to something that interests you, and see where it takes you." In college, Hoyt bought old cars, fixed them up, and sold them to classmates to help pay his tuition. After working on the Alaska pipeline, he entered the car business, working in dealerships and then at Ford Motor until he got a chance to buy his own dealership in 1990. He has had a good ride since then, making money, having fun, and not taking life too seriously.

I think these two very different examples of the septuagenarian shepherdess in the Italian Alps and the car dealer in modern day America make the same point. As we go about our days it's a good idea to have a sense that we are keeping company with life by getting close to things that capture our interest. Do that and you stand a good chance of finding real happiness.

### Rebalance to Restore

People who are fulfilled in their work tend to be fulfilled in their lives. They are, contrary to popular belief, not workaholics. Their love of work balances them out, as they tend to be equally serious about finding meaning in leisure.

## CRAFTING A LIFE

I know people who age gracefully because by engaging fully in all aspects of life they resolve not to allow their minds and bodies to atrophy. One such person is Dusty Johnstone, a friend and tennis partner, who formerly worked at IBM, while he and his wife raised four children. Eyeing retirement, Johnstone regularly skipped lunch and headed for the gym at the noon hour to work out and stay in shape. After leaving IBM, he was well prepared for his second "career," building himself and his wife a new house and coaching the cross country ski team at the local high school. Johnstone, who is now in his early 70's, trains regularly with the team, including taking his skiers for pre-season conditioning to the football stadium at Harvard, where, together, they run the steps in each section of the bleachers.

I suspect, like Johnstone, that there is a similar cohort of cancer patients who staunchly resist the prospect of dying. This thought occurred to me after my diagnosis five years ago with Non Hodgkins lymphoma. I began actively thinking about what I could do to slow, if not halt, the spread of the disease. I put additional stock in this notion after observing the now legendary case of the cyclist, Lance Armstrong.

When Armstrong was diagnosed with testicular cancer that subsequently traveled to his brain he discovered that his dire diagnosis suddenly clarified his life. In affirming his will to live, Armstrong drove himself to dedicate his life to its "highest and best use." That mindset transformed the curse of the disease into a blessing; an awakening and a goad to great feats. Armstrong subsequently won an astounding six Tours de France in a row.

By connecting with what he loved and did best, Armstrong

ultimately rebalanced his life which, I believe, helped restore his health. His triumphs served as testament to not just his cycling prowess, but to the power of a life made whole.

## **What's Free Can Only be Received**

Striving to reach our potential in any endeavor reminds us that our bodies and minds are our toughest, most versatile tools. Sadly, many people underuse them because they paid nothing for them and are, therefore, disinclined to invest in their upkeep. They take for granted what has been freely given.

It's important to see those things that come our way at no cost as gifts, and, therefore, as things that can only be received and can never be bought. Being able to graciously receive something is as much of a virtue as the ability to give generously. If you assume a receptive mindset then you will begin to properly value your body and your mind as the priceless possessions they are. Once you have that appreciation then investing in them comes easily, and at modest cost relative to the potential return.

Many humans have the biological potential to live to 90 or 100, but what most of us lack is the imagination and will to do so. And life, being hard, doesn't offer much help. A long life is the product of a vital, optimistic, disciplined, and resourceful mind. Mental spiritedness and longevity of the flesh go hand in hand.

Many people fail to exercise imagination because it takes hard work, particularly in the face of the inevitable adversity we meet along the way. Life beats us down and wears us out if we don't skillfully absorb and parry the negative energy coming at us. We can't just stand up to adversity; we have to outwit it.

# CRAFTING A LIFE

A good friend of mine grew up in a crowded urban household where the television was always on and where the adults were always smoking. Early on, she recognized this environment as alien and unnatural. So she resolved to spend much of her time engaged in activities that would transport her from what she knew to be a toxic environment. Her mother didn't drive, but that didn't stop my friend from riding her bike or taking the bus to her various athletic endeavors. (Barred as a girl from playing hockey, she masqueraded as a boy to make the team.) At home, she would play recordings of nature – thunderstorms, birdsongs, rushing water – to drown out the cacophony of the house and lull her to sleep. When it came time to apply for college, she was the one who researched colleges and arranged campus visits. Subsequently, she gained admission to Yale, Dartmouth, and Harvard.

When I look at this woman, now in her late 30's, I certainly see her as the sum of her accomplishments, achieved in the face of considerable odds. But I also see a woman who has retained her youthfulness, and youthful optimism, by always choosing to act in hopeful, creative, and non-fearing ways. That is no mean feat.

## Small Actions Heal Us

In contrast to this woman, many people, as they age, simply get tired and slowly give up. They then rationalize their loss of energy (inaction) by blaming forces beyond their control, such as genes. I know a man who is in his late 30's, and already a good 30 pounds overweight. He acknowledges his need to eat less and exercise more, but then he quickly adds that no male member of his family ever lived past 65, anyway. So, why bother? His fatalism frees him to continue down the path of least resistance.

I think that the idea that our genes are the masters of our fate is an overrated concept, perhaps because we Americans have become too accustomed to blaming, and now often suing, others for our setbacks. As a result, we have grown less willing to struggle for what we get and more willing to abdicate responsibility – even for our own health.

Genes are certainly *potential,* but they are not destiny. A person's true destiny lies in his outlook, his frame of mind. What matters is how clearly he sees himself and his place in the world, and how vigorously he moves to realize that vision. Seize each day and you will take ownership of your life. Genes as a determinant of fate will recede.

In *Saving Your Brain,* Jeff Victoroff, a neurologist and neuropsychiatrist, writes that in perhaps just five percent of Alzheimer's cases is the condition fully inherited. The majority of the time, Victoroff contends, the principal culprit is some sort of external insult in the form of disease, stress-induced behavior, toxicity, or trauma. Victoroff believes that we do things daily that injure our brains, from eating the wrong foods to losing our tempers to even thinking the wrong thoughts. I think he's on to something which will take years for science, moving methodically in search of quantitative proof, to bear out.

Nonetheless, the reason we hear so much in the media about stress is that we know, intuitively, if not empirically, that it can injure and even kill us. If that is the case, then it stands to reason that its antidotes – relaxed optimism, regular exercise, and a salutary approach to life – can safeguard health. Like Victoroff, I believe that there are many small actions we can take daily to heal, not wound, ourselves.

### Resist Resistance

Part of living healthfully involves a willingness to overcome resistance. Resistance mainly takes the form of fear or laziness. It is the default mode in many people, and part of our mission is to program it out of ourselves.

My experience as a writer has taught me that anything worth doing well will resist you. It will hold its secrets dear and play hard to get. A good piece of writing results mainly from a person's taking the initiative to show up daily and discipline his mind to concentrate on exactly what he is trying to say. The horror writer, Stephen King, has said that, "Writing equals ass in chair." The great non-fiction writer, John McPhee, used to roll out of bed in the morning and tie his bathrobe belt to the armrests of his chair to force himself to confront the blank page in his typewriter.

Quality of effort is an essential element of a person's life. Sincere and persistent effort breaks through that wall of resistance. It will let you into the inner circle of a problem or a pursuit to where its secrets lie, and where understanding becomes possible. When we sustain effort we reach a creative "tipping point" where its opposite, the resistance we have met, is no longer discouraging but suddenly turned doubly in our favor. This is akin to the second wind in sports, or the dawning of awareness that we merit for staying the course in any creative pursuit. Doors open if you lean against them long enough.

## Talking Keeps Us From Doing

Sustained effort pays dividends beyond the immediate tasks we take on. It leads a person to his philosophy of life, which evolves from his thoughts and actions, both large and small. Developing a philosophy of life should be done quietly. Do not announce to all within earshot what you are up to. Talking takes away from not just doing, but also becoming. It saps will and defocuses energy.

This is a fundamental idea of Buddhist teaching, and it conflicts sharply with the often boastful and self-promoting ways of the modern West. To the Buddhist, quietness is not secretiveness, nor is it necessarily modesty. It is rather a means of efficiently directing energy in order to ensure the best possible result. A painting, a piece of music, or a business plan only begins to take shape after we have put the requisite amount of solitary, conscientious time into it. It is the process – the enforced loneliness of artful doing – which does the creative work.

Once we have completed the job there will be plenty of time to tell the world, and the less we have diluted our efforts by talk the more boldly our accomplishments will speak for themselves. We will scarcely have to raise our voices.

## Make Boredom Fruitful

Focused effort also burns away boredom. Boredom, it goes without saying, is a none-too-hidden epidemic in a fast-paced modern world brimming with incessant appeals to the senses.

Try not to listen to people who see work as tedium and nothing but. Yes, as we come up we all do work that is "boring," and we certainly need to pay the bills and see to mundane chores. But the process of engaging fully in even simple tasks trains us to explore work's potential. Getting into that habit will eventually guide a person toward his true calling, and from there on out he will never be bored.

In *The Conquest of Happiness* Bertrand Russell identifies two types of boredom. One he calls "stultifying," and the other "fructifying." In distinguishing them, Russell writes: "The fructifying kind arises from the absence of drugs, and the stultifying from the absence of vital activities." Russell's point is that in any creative effort there is a certain amount of repetitive and even monotonous work. But it is through our ability to identify a task we deem vital and then stay with it that we begin to explore its bounds. We transform something that is potentially stultifying to an activity that is unambiguously fruitful.

### Don't Be Boring and the World Won't Bore You

If you own a dog then perhaps you have heard the adage, "There are no bad dogs, only bad dog owners." Something analogous might be said on the subject of boredom: "There is no boredom. There are only boring people."

I recall a few years back traveling with my older son who at that stage in his life was a moody teenager. We were out on San Juan Island in the Pacific Northwest on a sparkling June day. I wanted to stop by a sculpture park at the end of the island. My son began to grumble at this prospect, and by the time we arrived at our destination he was on my case about how "boring" this sidetrip was. After a certain amount of whining on his part, I blew up, telling him all I wanted to do was spend a few minutes walking around a beautiful place on a beautiful day.

Chastened, my son returned to the car in silence. On the way back, a small insect flew in the car window and landed on his arm. It immediately caught his attention, and he began to intently study this insect. I was amazed how engrossed my son became in this activity. This went on for a few minutes until the insect flew back out the window. Peace had definitely been restored.

The next day we went out in a kayak to look for whales. After paddling for three hours, and with my son exuding nothing but enthusiasm, I began to fret. What if we didn't see a whale? How disappointed would he then be? An hour later, we spotted a small pod of whales and began paddling toward them. As we advanced, they kept coming our way, until they breached barely 20 yards from the boat and proceeded to glide right under us. Later, our guide would confide to us that he had never before been that close to a pod of whales.

I couldn't help thinking that these two events, one subtle, the other dramatic, were somehow connected. My son, by surrendering his attention – and his angst – to the insect that had alighted on his arm, had chosen to make his boredom fruitful. The next day, nature would reward his wise choice in emphatic fashion.

### Produce From Your Own Resources

I became a personal coach to satisfy two aims. First, I wanted to play a direct and positive role in the lives of other people by listening to them and offering my thoughts, based on my 50-plus years of living. Second, I wanted to engage in a form of thinking and writing that meant something to me.

For more than 25 years prior to becoming a coach I had made my living as a journalist, and in that time the profession I had happily entered had shifted around me. It had become less meaningful as the emphasis on entertainment and surface over substance and depth had increased. Being a journalist no longer felt to me like the important calling it was when I started out. It was time for a change.

It was time to embark on a new, more genuine course. The choice, despite whatever attendant risks it held – there was no definable "market" or audience; I would simply be hanging out my shingle and finding clients as I went – nonetheless, seemed obvious to me because it felt right. That was what really mattered.

Each of us holds a unique wisdom, which means that each of us has something important to reveal to the world and teach others. For some people it can take the better part of a lifetime to discern that talent within, not to mention shape it into a calling. Many others may never find it because they are lost in a role scripted by others or by circumstances that demand that they do things that do not truthfully reflect who they are. Finding the courage to say "No" to others and "Yes" to ourselves can be daunting. It is always easier, as Seneca puts it, to "wander aimlessly" because a life without clear goals demands little accountability. On the other hand, once we have announced our intent to achieve a specific goal we put ourselves on the line. We have raised the stakes. That can scare a lot of people off.

But when we choose, as Seneca writes, "to follow a track," or as Montaigne puts it, "get on the straight and open road," we connect who we are with what we are meant to be. Character becomes destiny. The quest to discover that special skill of ours – and, by extension, that special person we are – is a vital one in the literal sense of that word. It is life-giving. Don't be afraid to act; don't be afraid to take a risk or make a mistake. If you do nothing, then nothing will be your reward. Even worse, events will act upon you. Life will happen to you.

The object in life is for the individual to happen to life, through the energetic exercise of his faculties. We need to make a mark and forge our destinies; to move beyond mouthing truths to living them. "But in the case of a grown man who has made incontestable progress it is disgraceful to go hunting after gems of wisdom and prop himself up with a minute number of the best-known sayings," warns Seneca. "He should be delivering himself of such sayings, not memorizing them. Assume authority yourself and utter something that may be handed down to posterity. Produce something from your own resources."

### Make it Look Easy

We might think of the accomplished person as a well-made building. There is much that escapes the eye; the scaffolding once erected to raise the structure, the complex inner workings that allow it to stand and function. Most people observing a masterpiece fail to reflect on, much less empathize with, the artist's toil and anguish in creating it.

One of the raps against the successful person is that "they

## CRAFTING A LIFE

make it look easy," as if somehow this is a crime. The truth is that those who make it look easy put in a lot of hard work behind the scenes, and this effort often goes unnoticed. To be sure, there are people who are born with a particular gift, but even those people will suffer if they fail to cultivate their talent. Unfulfilled potential can lead to a lifetime of persistently gnawing regret.

The whole idea, in fact, is to make it look easy – to become a graceful person in the eyes of others – because grace is the signature of sincere effort. It signifies talent recognized, and talent respected.

Roger Federer is one of the most gifted tennis players in the history of the sport. He has every shot in the book, and he executes each with a classic grace. But Federer didn't receive the full respect of the tennis community until he disciplined his manifold gifts and converted them into tangible results in his 2003 season when he won Wimbledon, won titles on four different surfaces, and finished ranked second in the world. (His accomplishments the following year dwarfed those. In 2004, Federer won three of the four Grand Slam events and a total of ten major tournaments.) Anyone who watched Federer during that run could not help but notice that his will and fight were every bit as evident as his grace. In fact, the former helped shape the latter.

Before his ascent to the top of men's tennis, Federer was known as a very talented player with great promise. Now, he is widely respected as a man who has channeled that talent by enlisting true effort in its service. He is known quite simply as perhaps the greatest player in the history of the game because he has done the hard work to make his genius real.

# TRUE SPIRIT, TRUE SELF

## Push Luck Away

Another complaint one often hears about a person experiencing success is that he "just got lucky." Envy, which produces such sentiment, is a toxic emotion. It should be discounted in others and discouraged in oneself.

Just as life is not fair, luck is not equally apportioned. But the more you work to negate luck's impact, by neither expecting it nor relying on it, the less of a factor it becomes in your success. And yet, when luck does come your way it will smile all the more on you.

You have to push luck away by replacing it with hard and honest work to ultimately get it back in your corner. "Luck," as we tend to call it, is ultimately apportioned more to the good than to the lucky. "When you're good you get lucky," is an expression I have heard on occasion from my brother-in-law, an accomplished actor who came up the hard way. Arriving in New York some 40 years ago with little money in his pocket and a lot of desire in his heart, he worked on the docks by day and attended auditions at night. His struggles and sacrifices over many years eventually bore fruit in the form of a successful career on Broadway and later in Hollywood. He surely earned whatever "luck" came his way.

Conversely, when we take our good fortune for granted or see it as an entitlement it will eventually go against us. It is a karmic credit that turns into a karmic debt. It is energy that will migrate to where it is more appreciated and will be put to better use. If a person is blessed with native talent, and he doesn't develop it, then by definition he is squandering it. And in time his life will look anything but easy. It is important to recognize that whatever gifts we enter this life with are precious. We must use them wisely. If we don't, they will simply vanish.

**Quiet Hands Are Grateful Hands**

How then do we become more mindful of our good fortune? How do we turn it to full advantage?

It's important to have a sense of gratitude as the backdrop of not just your thinking but the flow of your life. Be mindful each day of what you have by taking time out to inventory the good. If you suffer a reversal, or feel victimized by another person, take some time to stew over the problem and then formulate a positive remedy. After that, let it go, move on with your day, engaging in something that stokes, not saps, your energy. If and when it comes time to revisit and deal with the earlier problem, you are prepared to address it with a fresh mind.

Gratitude is such a vital frame of mind because it is so easy to take good things for granted. People who have too many things and treat their possessions and gifts cavalierly court eventual poverty – if not of the pocketbook, then of the soul. Conversely, the man who knows what he has and uses it well will never be poor. With gratitude as our guide and grounding, the dynamic of our lives turns around. Instead of grasping after things that only respond by eluding us, things come to us because they sense and appreciate our thankful natures.

In *Inner Tennis: Playing the Game,* Tim Gallwey writes about the delicate link between mind and muscle: "Trusting the body is the first principle of the Inner Game of sports," writes Gallwey. "The second is quieting the mind. The capacity of our bodies to perform at their highest potential is in direct proportion to the stillness of our minds. When the mind is noisy, anxious, and distracted, it interferes with the nervous system's silent instructions to the muscles. It's like static in the communication system; the subtler messages get drowned out, and there is little subtlety in the body's motion."

Tennis players speak of "soft" or "quiet" hands as an attribute. Quiet hands gain a good feel for the ball and in turn can feed back that information in nuanced form to the mind. The truer the data coming back to the brain then the more smoothly the muscles will function.

Soft hands in life cultivate a receptive mind – and vice versa. A receptive mind is a calm, observant, and learning mind.

It is important to live and work with quiet – non-grasping – hands. Let that trait flow into all areas of your life, and your fair share of good things will flow your way. Remember that the vitals such as air and water – the most abundant yet also the most precious of all things – cannot be held at all. They can only be received.

But quiet, open hands can at least cradle whatever they touch. Quiet hands are intelligent hands. They inform the whole person. When Seneca writes that "a way of speaking which is restrained, not bold, suits a wise man in the same way as an unassuming sort of walk does," he is really talking about all facets of a life. If you infuse your life with a sense of gratitude then you will act with restraint. Act with restraint and you will become so much more aware of the world around you because the world, sensing your gentle demeanor, will readily open itself to you.

## Step Outside Yourself

A sense of quiet gratitude is the vital backdrop to good health. Calmness in mind inspires vigor in body. Together, they buffer a person from life's inevitable stresses. Once we are in touch with what it means to practice good health we don't want to let it go. It feels too good.

If we commit to practicing healthy exertion we will find ways to spend more time outdoors. We will realize that nature is our birthplace and being connected to it is our birthright. Aside from such obvious tonics as fresh air and sunshine, the outdoors offers other benefits. These include:

- *When you are outside your perspective comes into balance.* You see and sense the feminine curves of nature, which are markedly different from the straight lines and linear feel of the *manmade* world.

- *When you step outside you step outside yourself.* You move beyond the confines of the ego, which is to say that nature puts us in our place, where we are meant to be if we are to live the healthiest of lives. One element of a significant life is an awareness of one's relative insignificance in the larger world.

- *The outdoors is our native venue.* In *The Conquest of Happiness,* Bertrand Russell describes the primitive delight of a two-year old boy "who had been kept in London and taken out for the first time to walk in green country." Even though it was a wet and muddy winter's day the boy exulted as he buried his face in the wet grass. Observing this, Russell noted, "Whatever we may wish to think, we are creatures of Earth; our life is part of the life of the earth, and we draw our nourishment from it just as the plants and animals do. The rhythm of Earth life is slow; autumn and winter are as essential to it as spring and summer, and rest is as essential as motion. To the child, even more to the man, it is necessary to preserve some contact with the ebb and flow of terrestrial life. The human body has been adapted through the ages to this rhythm."

### Live Timelessly

Adopt a similar mindset as it relates to time. Strive to create and practice timelessness in your life. Avoid a rigid schedule, and try not to wear a watch. Work hard when you have the energy. When you feel hungry, eat; when you feel sleepy, rest. That will slow down time, allowing it to be savored and valued.

"Managing" time is really about allowing it to merge into the backdrop of your life. It is not about compulsively keeping a schedule. That only ends up chopping time into small bits that drift away before our eyes. Strive to keep time in one piece by living so one activity flows into the next, binding your days into an unbroken strand you can happily call a life.

### Accept the Impermanence of Life

When we live closer to nature's rhythms we begin to understand a strange conundrum. We are mortal, and life is short. The earth

## CRAFTING A LIFE

and the universe are forever. In other words, the evident impermanence of our lives lies locked within the timeless void of existence. When we see our lives in such stark relief we begin to value every day. Life is short, and the only remedy is to make it sweet. Grateful awareness becomes the ambient energy coursing through our lives.

The grateful man doesn't just appreciate the preciousness of the moment. He understands it. He stops looking ahead and grasping in the present in an effort to secure a future that will always remain uncertain. He simply lives now. If he does so with sincerity, honesty, and kindness then the universe will meet his true needs and honor his soul.

We, therefore, stand the best chance of securing the future by living in the present as fully and mindfully and thankfully as we possibly can. When we acknowledge the impermanence of life we stand the best chance of living lives that are long, full, and enduring.

# AFTERWORD

One impression that I would like to leave with readers is my belief in the power, dignity, and worth of the individual. And from that belief flows the possibility of liberation, not just for the self, but for all people and all creatures.

Just as all things begin and end at a single point, the world in the final analysis is simply a composite, distilled reflection of how each of us lives his or her respective life. If we find our world lacking then we need look inside and begin the process of change from there. It is all we can do, and it is what we should do.

The way back, for individual humans and for the planet we inhabit, as any great journey, begins with a single step – taken singly. It is true that that first step requires insight and courage, but it is equally true that each step thereafter grows progressively easier and more effortless. Wisdom creates its own momentum, as urgent as it is pleasurable. Once embarked on the right path, we come to realize that there is really no other way. The practice of goodness, which flows from a commitment to wise living, is not only an easy habit to get into, but a natural one.

While we never reach our ultimate goal, that is precisely the point. Process, practice, "the journey" are what matter, and by focusing on them to the exclusion of goals and outcomes we light the path. We light the path not just for ourselves, but by ourselves. Others will look to us, acknowledge, and quietly follow.

I began this book writing about the inherently dichotomous nature of human experience. The wise journey is one that transcends this paradox. The well-lived life moves past the oppositional natures of good and evil, man and woman, action and reaction. It negates our fixation with "winning" and "losing." It leads us, rather, into the more promising and open terrain of truthful living. Truthful living seeks harmony in all things, and between all things. From perfect balance we live directed, unified lives graced with courage, strength, and love.

If we commit ourselves to living truthfully then we receive wisdom for ourselves and offer peace to the world. We can give, nor receive, no greater gift.

# SUGGESTED READING

Aristotle, *Ethics*, London: Penguin Books, 1976.

Aurelius, Marcus, *Meditations*, Ware, England: Wordsworth, 1997.

Bell, Derrick, *Ethical Ambition: Living a Life of Meaning and Worth*, New York: Bloomsbury, 2003.

Branden, Nathaniel, *Honoring the Self: The Psychology of Confidence and Respect*, New York: Bantam, 1985.

Branden, Nathaniel, *Taking Responsibility: Self-Reliance and the Accountable Life*, New York: Fireside, 1996.

Carse, James P., *Finite and Infinite Games: A Vision of Life as Play and Possibility*, New York: The Free Press, 1986.

Chaudhuri, Haridas, *The Essence of Spiritual Philosophy*, New Delhi: HarperCollins/Indus, 1992.

Chödrön, Pema, *Start Where You Are: A Guide to Compassionate Living*, Boston: Shambhala, 1994.

Csikszentmihalyi, Mihaly, *Flow: The Psychology of Optimal Experience*, New York: HarperPerennial, 1991.

Csikszentmihalyi, Mihaly, *The Evolving Self: A Psychology for the Third Millennium*, New York: HarperPerennial, 1994.

De Montaigne, Michel, *Essays*, London: Penguin, 1993.

Emerson, Ralph Waldo, *Self-Reliance and Other Essays*, New York: Dover, 1993.

Epictetus, *Enchiridion*, Amherst, New York: Prometheus, 1991.

Gallwey, W. Timothy, *Inner Tennis: Playing the Game*, New York: Random House, 1976.

Gates, Rolf and Katrina Kenison, *Meditations from the Mat: Daily Reflections on the Path of Yoga*, New York: Anchor, 2002.

Henri, Robert, *The Art Spirit*, Oxford: Westview/Icon, 1984.

Hoffer, Eric, *The True Believer: Thoughts on the Nature of Mass Movements*, New York: HarperPerennial, 1989.

Jung, C.G., *The Undiscovered Self*, Princeton, New Jersey: Princeton/Bollingen, 1990.

Loehr, James E., *The Mental Game: Winning at Pressure Tennis*, New York: Penguin/Plume, 1991.

Marinoff, Lou, *Therapy for the Sane: How Philosophy Can Change Your Life*, New York: Bloomsbury, 2004.

# SUGGESTED READING

Maslow, Abraham H., *Toward a Psychology of Being: Second Edition,* New York: Van Nostrand Reinhold, 1968.

Penick, Harvey with Bud Shrake, *Harvey Penick's Little Red Book: Lessons and Teachings from a Lifetime in Golf,* New York: Fireside, 1999.

Rand, Ayn, *The Voice of Reason: Essays in Objectivist Thought,* New York: Penguin/Meridian, 1990.

Rilke, Rainer Maria, *Letters to a Young Poet,* New York: W.W. Norton, 1993.

Russell, Bertrand, *The Conquest of Happiness,* New York: Liveright, 1996.

Seneca, *Letters From a Stoic,* London: Penguin, 1969.

Strunk, William Jr., and E.B. White, *The Elements of Style: Third Edition,* New York: Macmillan, 1979.

Suzuki, Shunryu, *Zen Mind, Beginner's Mind: Informal Talks on Zen Meditation and Practice,* New York: Weatherhill, 1994.

Thondup, Tulku, *The Healing Power of Mind: Simple Meditation Exercises for Health, Well-Being, and Enlightenment,* Boston: Shambhala, 1998.

Thoreau, Henry David, *Walden,* Boston: Houghton Mifflin, 1964.

# NOTES

# TRUE SPIRIT, TRUE SELF

# NOTES

# TRUE SPIRIT, TRUE SELF

# ABOUT THE AUTHOR

An award-winning journalist for the past 25 years, Ed Welles was a senior writer at *Inc.* magazine for 13 years and a staff writer at *West*, the Sunday magazine of *The San Jose Mercury News* for six years. In 1995, he was a finalist for a National Magazine Award, and in 1987 he won a Gerald Loeb Award, the most sought after U.S. prize in business and economic journalism. In 2005 he was a finalist for the prestigious Business Journalist of the Year Awards in the United Kingdom. Welles has also written for the *The Washington Post*, *The Boston Globe*, *Audubon Magazine*, *National Geographic* and *Fortune Small Business*.

He is now a personal coach specializing in working with motivated individuals in midlife, helping them re-tool their thinking to choose new careers, deepen their lives, and take on new challenges. He lives in Lake Placid, NY.

To inquire or learn more about his services please visit his website at *www.vital-mind.com*